A Widow's Hope

Praise for *A Widow's Hope*

Rivaled by her subjective suffering as a widow, from the onset of the book, from the very first sentence, the author endearingly empathizes with widowers, meticulously prepares widowers on precisely what to expect in the bereavement process, and offers holistic prescriptions to assist widowers on their road to healing that will ultimately produce a healthy prognosis. BRAVO!

Dr. Juan Gerardo Galván-Rodríguez, psychotherapist and clinical director, Holy Family Psychotherapy Training Institute

Julie Ortiz has not only dealt with her own traumatic grievances, but understands how to connect with her audience through empathy and realness. I'm proud of this work, and I can see it helping so many people who have experienced tragic loss and need a guide to get them through the fragile healing process.

Elisa Escalante, LCSW, OEF veteran, author of *Unseen: Uncovering the Invisible Wounds of Military Trauma*

Brilliant and sobering. Julie Ortiz takes readers on an extraordinary, open, and honest journey through personal tragedy and the grieving process. *A Widow's Hope* is a must-read for those seeking a guide and companionship from an author who has experienced surviving the loss of a loved one. From survival mode and physical/mental health to spirituality and helping children through the grieving process, *A Widow's Hope* has it all.

Dr. P. Mumphrey, EdS, MS, US Army veteran, teacher

In *A Widow's Hope*, Julie Ortiz tells with emotional honesty the story of her interior desolation after her husband's tragic death and her journey toward healing. As someone who accompanied Julie through part of her ordeal, I can personally attest to the admirable courage and fidelity she showed in many difficult situations. May her story and the practical knowledge she has acquired provide assistance, consolation, and hope to those in like circumstances.

Fr. Joseph Pilsner, CSB, professor of Theology

A Widow's Hope: A Guide for Widows in Survival Mode by Julie Escalante Ortiz is a raw and gut wrenching phenomenological account of trauma and complex grief from a widower's perspective. Mrs. Ortiz explores the depth of emotions and existential crisis that accompanies this all too often experience for young wives and mothers. Many widowers will find connection and permission to sift through some very difficult and often shame producing thoughts and emotions without judgement, because of the courageous nature of Mrs. Ortiz's narrative. In addition, Mrs. Ortiz provides readers with a path for hope and healing through genuine connection and faith. This is a must read for widowers, but it is also an essential read for those who wish to support widowers.

Dr. Harris Ty Leonard, Ph.D., LPC-S, professor of Counseling, University of Mary Hardin-Baylor

Julie Escalante Ortiz

A Widow's *Hope*

A GUIDE FOR WIDOWS IN SURVIVAL MODE

NEW YORK

LONDON • NASHVILLE • MELBOURNE • VANCOUVER

A Widow's Hope

A Guide for Widows in Survival Mode

© 2023 Julie Escalante Ortiz

Published in New York, New York, by Morgan James Publishing. Morgan James is a trademark of Morgan James, LLC. www.MorganJamesPublishing.com

Proudly distributed by Ingram Publisher Services.

Scriptures are taken from the KING JAMES VERSION (KJV): KING JAMES VERSION, public domain.

ISBN 9781631959745 paperback
ISBN 9781631959752 ebook
Library of Congress Control Number:
2022938647

Cover & Interior Design by:
Christopher Kirk
www.GFSstudio.com

Morgan James is a proud partner of Habitat for Humanity Peninsula and Greater Williamsburg. Partners in building since 2006.

Get involved today! Visit MorganJamesPublishing.com/giving-back

Table Of Contents

Acknowledgments

A Special Thank You . . .

Thank you to my dear widows and widowers. There is a deep need in our widow community, and my hope, my driving-force, to finish this book has always been to serve you all with this work of love. Allowing yourself to grieve is loving yourself. If no one else in your life is telling you this, I pray you will hear me say it to you: *I am so proud of you.* This is the hardest obstacle you will ever survive. And I pray my love reaches you.

Thank You to Our Dearest Children

Thank you, Daniella, for your love, kindness, and selfless love to each of your family members. You are brilliant, funny, and beautiful. You share in your father's love of science, art, music, and above all, your faith, which is so evident in your big, selfless heart.

Thank you, Gabriel, for your love, inquisitive mind, and unique spirituality. You are brilliant, silly, have a profound love for nature, and can totally beat me in video games any day! You share in your father's love of art, faith, and science like no one I have ever met!

Thank you, Tony, for your love, hilarious sense of humor, and selfless kindness. You are brilliant, hilarious, and the best chef in the family! You share in your father's love of science, natural curiosity in conducting science experiments, equally magnetic personality, and your delicious cooking skills!

Thank You to My Beloved Family

Rene, Esther, Angelica, Mario, Mom, Dad, Lisa, Natalie, Nicole, Jonathan, Marina, Michelle, and our beloved Fr. Joseph Pilsner, CSB. Thank you fellow author—also my cousin—Elisa Escalante for encouraging me to be brave and pursue publishing.

And finally, thank you to Morgan James Publishing, a new type of family, for believing in the value of this message.

Gabe's Prayer

Gabe: Dear God, help us do your work.
Mom: What is God's work, Gabriel?
Gabe: To be loving.

Introduction

I am sorry you had to buy this book. Your world has now changed forever. It has been flipped upside down and you don't know who you are anymore, much less where you are going. You haven't even begun to process the loss of your soulmate, the loss of your identity, the loss of your friends, and maybe even the loss of your faith. Life as you knew it is gone forever. This traumatic experience has plucked you from your normal routine with a normal family and tossed you into survival mode—treading water upon the raging waves as they try to wash you under, and there's no lifeboat in sight.

The only thing you need to hear right now is nothing. There is not one thing you can hear in the whole wide world that will comfort you. What you need is, not words, but arms to hold you, shoulders for you to cry on, ears to listen to you, and your children to hold and kiss you. You need someone to just sit with you, not try to "understand" your pain. Sure, I could tell you what you've already heard a hundred times by now: "Take one day at a time," or, "Just breathe," or, "It just takes time," but I know as much as any widow that you don't need to hear that again. There are some losses in life in which there is no end to our grief. I wish someone had told me this as a young widow of just twenty-nine years old with three little children aged three, five, and seven.

There are many books about widowhood and grief. Though those books are helpful when the time is right, the shock and the aftermath of such a traumatic experience can make it difficult to find the time and motivation to read them while surviving the daily obstacles that zap your energy. Right now, you're too busy surviving funeral planning, endless calls and texts from family, tireless efforts to obtain the death certificate, meetings with social security, arrangements to settle debts, and all the calls to banks, mortgagors, employers, and more. Not to mention the practical things, like ensuring the children have been fed, arranging who will take them to school while you pick out the casket, or helping your children with things only *you* can help with. And then it hits you: "How will I even tell them that their father is dead? They don't even know what 'dead' means!" Just thinking of the unending list of things to be done can leave you feeling smothered and breathless. Now is not the time for a novel. Now is the time for a survival book, because right now, that's what you are doing—*surviving*.

The following chapters are only a fellow widow's experience combined with practical advice for surviving the next months of this new life. You will hear me say many times throughout this book that it is not healthy to tell someone else how to grieve. I am not attempting to do this. I am merely sharing my story of walking through the dark valley while sharing the ways that I dug my way out of the trenches and back to the land of the living. Do not let anyone tell you how to grieve. At the end of the day, we all will choose a path. What works for some may be painful for others, and vice versa.

Also, for those of you reading this because you are close to a widow or widower, please understand that many widowed people feel paralyzed in their grief and may lack the motivation to read anything at present, much less work through the grieving process. Some may not even be aware that there is anything to heal within themselves and may prefer to stay where they are despite being in a painful state of denial and avoidance. If that's the case, you might be the one benefiting from reading this so you can share the information with them the best way you know how. I remember the first time someone gave me a book after my loss—I wanted to spit! But when the time was right, it was there. Please keep in mind that no one can force healing. The widow has to be in a place of such great pain that the pain of staying where they are is greater than the potential pain of moving forward with their grieving process. When they get to that place, you will be ready to give them this book.

To My Javier

My dearest love, it has taken me nine years to complete this part of the book. I wrote all the other chapters before this one and just left this part blank because the pain was too great. Here I am, nine years later, staring at the page, and I still can't find the words. How do I put into words the details of your last breaths? As I grapple with the death occurring inside of me from the death of you, I am having to ask you to help me write these words for us because I can't seem to find the strength. So now I imagine your big, strong hand holding mine. I imagine you leading my pen across this page soaked in tears.

I wish I could go back in time and change February 9, 2013. Oh, the countless times I lay daydreaming of warning you and your coworker Mike of the horrific nightmare that was about to unfold at that chemical plant that morning. You weren't even supposed to work that day, but you were going in as a favor. I vividly remember waking groggily to a crack in the door as light poured into our dark bedroom. You came in and said your goodbye the same way you had a million times before. You leaned down over me, kissed me, and said, "I filled up your car's tank and I charged your phone. See you in a few hours, babe. I love you." I sleepily replied, "I love you, baby, be careful," as I always did. I listened to the heavy steps of your work boots steadily fade down the hallway and out the door. God, help me! If only I had jumped out of bed and thrown my arms around your neck and never let you go . . .

SECTION 1:
Survival Mode

Chapter 1

Picking Out the Tombstone—
Surviving the Funeral

My dearest love, I sit here with my dad. I have just learned it is to be a closed-casket funeral. It didn't register exactly what that meant at first because my brain is lagging from exhaustion and takes minutes to catch up. This news buckles me over in agony, and despite heaving deep breaths into my lungs, I still feel like I'm suffocating: "Wait! I won't be able to see him? I won't be able to say goodbye?" The funeral home staff look with eyes full of pity at the withered, frail twenty-nine-year-old mother standing before them and reply, "No. I'm so sorry."

How could I be this slow to realize this? How could I just now grasp that, because you died in an explosion, your wife and children will have nothing to say goodbye to? I feel like I've been robbed all over again. We all have. To have a final goodbye and look down upon your face one last time as you lie in your casket has been carrying me through these days. My love, how will I endure life without seeing you again? Hearing your voice? Smelling your hair? Feeling your touch?

I am led into a room where I am shown a variety of caskets—bronze, gold, metallic, wooden—all lined with satin. It seems too difficult a task. Do I choose a gold or silver casket? I instinctually grab my phone to call you because you are always the one I call when I am faced with difficult decisions, but I can't ask you to help with this one. The funeral director now asks me if I would like to engrave a photo of you on the top of your casket. My esophagus burns from swallowing down my stomach's contents for the tenth time since breakfast. The director asks which casket I would like. In my mind, I overturn and hurl all the caskets, screaming "NO!" as I run out of the building, pulling out my hair in sheer madness.

Suddenly, I snap back to reality as the funeral director asks again, "Ms. Ortiz? Which casket would you like to choose?" I respond, "We'll take this one. I think he would like this casket." Then he leads my shell of a person into the next room to pick out your tombstone. Hmm, do I add a picture on your headstone or not? I cannot believe I am even asking myself this question! Is this real life? This has to be a nightmare. This agony cannot be imagined, but here I am, living it. I visualize taking out my brain because I need rest from the incessant churning of my mind. As we sit down to plan your funeral, I am at a loss for words at the ease at which the director proceeds to discuss the details of my husband's funeral, as if we were planning an event! I come to another agonizing realization: I will actually have to be present. How? My love, how in this world will I survive your funeral without you?

I think back to the recent painful funerals of both of our grandmothers earlier this year and how much I depended on your strong shoulders to cry on, hold me up, and support me when I felt weak. This pain has not yet been realized by my psyche, and perhaps that is the only saving grace that will see me through your funeral.

Looking into our children's eyes, I cannot believe that you will never hold them again. You will never hide from them during hide-and-seek, play nerf-gun wars, dance with your daughter, teach your sons how to change a tire or throw a baseball, teach them your hobby of woodworking, watch them walk across the stage on college graduation day, or walk your daughter down the aisle on their wedding day! Even the little things, like helping them with their organic chemistry or trigonometry homework; you're the chemist, not me!

How could I ever replace all that you are? Who am I now if I am not your wife? I do not want to be a widow at twenty-nine years old! I don't want to be a single mom! What are we now if we are not a "whole" family? I want my old life back! I met you when I was eighteen—my first boyfriend, my first everything! And here I am, eleven years later, burying you! I don't want to accept this as my life. A life, quite frankly, of hell on earth. There is no going back in time. You are gone forever, and so am I.

Hold me up today, my dearest love, I beg you. God, help me!

*D*ear fellow widow or widower, the day I buried the love of my life, I could not imagine my life without him. Just as you cannot live without your spouse. I first met him at the young age of eighteen while living in the dormitories at Our Lady of the Lake University in San Antonio. Twenty years later, I am a completely different human being. Although I am not a mental health professional, I am a fellow widow. I am sorry that you are now a member of this club that no one wants to belong to. I will never forget the first time I checked the "widowed" box in the marital status section of a form. Even obtaining the title "widow" made me feel disgusted with my life and was just one more thing added to the mountain of things that I had to grieve.

My hope is to help other widows by sharing my story and the steps I took to survive these nine years as a widow.

Grief from tremendous loss is a lifelong journey because there are some losses in life in which there is no end to grief. In all these years, the best way I can describe the pain of grief is like a two-ton boulder being dropped on your shoulders. Over the passing years, the weight of this painful burden doesn't get any *lighter*—we widows merely grow *stronger*. This grieving process takes time and strategic measures to regain a new sense of self, purpose, and meaning; a process which I have laid out in this guide with the specific steps I took to healthily grieve, heal, cope, and live again.

Chapter 2

How Do I Tell Them Daddy is Dead?

My dearest love, today was the second-worst day of my life. I told our children you are dead. I still cannot believe we both died yesterday. I asked my father to help me break the news to our babies.

We all sat in our living room, our little babies' sweet, meek doe eyes looking up at me while they sat in their grandfather's arms. I clenched my teeth, felt my gut flip-flop as if I were free-falling, and begged you to help me find the words to tell our three-year-old, five-year-old, and seven-year-old that you are dead. It took every remaining ounce of strength I had within me to utter the words to our little lambs that you were gone forever. I felt physically ill not knowing how they would react to the news that their Daddy, their Super-man, their Pappa Bear, is dead—never to be seen, held, or touched again. I squeezed them tight as I whispered out these words, "My darlings, yesterday there was an explosion at Daddy's work, and now he is dead and in Heaven." Our timid, soft-natured seven-year-old daughter—Daddy's little girl—began to violently kick and scream, "NO! NO!" It took the breath right out of my father and me. It felt as though it had aged us at least a decade, and my soul felt as if it had risen out of my body. Like me, our daughter could not accept it.

It was equally heartbreaking and traumatizing for us to witness our boys just sitting there with their innocent, blank faces and vacant, sad eyes. It was obvious that they could not compute what they had been told. Our precious three-year-old Tony asked me, "Mommy, what's 'dead'?"

My love, I am in hell. Where did you go? How are you gone? How can this be our life now? How could life be so cruel?

*T*he days leading up to the funeral were a blur. The phone calls and cards piled up in mountainous pro-portions. My face was an expressionless, vacant stare as family from California, close and distant friends, neighbors, coworkers, and—the hardest of all—Javier's co-workers from the chemical plant all came to console the inconsolable. My own friends and family did not know how to speak to me.

As I sat, zoned-out in my pain, the doorbell rang unceasingly as my family greeted those bringing meals, volunteers cutting my grass, men fixing things around our house, and friends dropping off gifts for the children on Valentine's Day.

There were so many times I wanted to tell everyone to leave because I felt ill. My head was splitting from a constant migraine and having little to no sleep in over a week. I had just told my children their daddy is dead, and people were proceeding to tell me the ingredients in the casserole. As I listened to the casserole conversation, I visualized running out of the house to who knows where . . . just running. I suddenly understood the scene in *Forrest Gump* when Forrest decided to just run and run and never stop. Perhaps I would run and never stop too. Then I snapped back to reality as the sound of their voice rose to a question. "Yes, ma'am," I replied, as I nodded and forced a smile. Did I just smile? How could I smile? Was I forgetting him already?

However, nothing could prepare me for the deafening silence that would follow after the calls and visits stopped. Nothing could prepare me for the bleak house of dismal solitude and loneliness. I was twenty-nine years old, at the prime of my youth, yet I felt as though I were already dead inside. Strangers in support groups would tell me, "Oh, you're young! You'll be fine!" But when I was around my peers, I didn't feel young at all. I felt I had aged mentally and physically by at least twenty years. I had never felt more lost and alone. With each passing moment, the loneliness, isolation, and immense weight of grief became harder to endure, as if I was being repeatedly struck by a heavyweight champion boxer.

It is quite clear to all those surrounding a widow that she is in survival mode, however, it may not be so apparent to the widow. Nor does it dawn on anyone involved just how long that survival mode lasts. Most assume that it is an initial shock that soon wears off over time. This book will paint the true picture of the reality that a widow endures. The widow may feel bombarded by the jackhammer of questions, become numb, paralyzed, and even unable to respond. This is when close loved ones can step up to organize practical help and care for the widow and her children (organizing meals, cleaning, providing childcare, and more).

Friends and family often flood the widow with attempts to make them feel better. Please hear this: there are no words, so don't speak. There is nothing more important than a quiet, steadfast presence. A presence that proves to be there, not just initially, but over and over again. Perhaps indefinitely. Now is the time to listen, care, love, support, and above all, simply just be there.

Chapter 3

Six Feet Under

My dearest love, I sit here at your graveside as our children's godfather, our beloved Father Pilsner, attempts to console us in his final words of your burial service. I try to take in all the details of your casket to feel your earthly presence one last time before you are lowered six feet under into the earth.

The undertakers might as well lower me with you because I feel dead. Even though it is senseless, I do not want to let your casket go. It feels as though my body lies within it too. After all, isn't that what we are? "One flesh?" I cannot believe my eyes will never take you in again.

As the undertakers begin to lower you into the earth, I cannot hold my pain in any longer. I release a wail from

deep within my soul as our children cry out, "DADDY!"
and my entire family erupts into tears. Tears even roll down
the cheeks of the undertakers; no wonder they are wearing
sunglasses. My heart feels as though it has burst out of my
chest and has atrophied to stone. I try to force myself to be
comforted in knowing that you are with God, but it's hard
to see past the pain. My mind feels like it's dwelling in a
dark void . . . six feet under. Why can't I feel anything? It
is because the unforgiving abyss has swallowed up the old
Julie and only her shell remains. God, don't leave me. I
need You. Please help me, God.

*T*rauma inflicts lifelong invisible wounds. I will never forget the first moment the shock began to subside ever so slightly, and the veil was lifted just enough for me to grasp the traumatic reality of my life as a young widow. Realities like when I was told early in the morning that my husband and his close friend/coworker were trapped inside a building due to an explosion at the chemical plant. And when I was told by firemen and police to go into a safe building nearby as I stood outside the fiery inferno and questioned why they weren't going inside to save them. And when I was asked harrowing questions like, "Can you get his dental records to ID his body?" And when I told my children their daddy was dead. And when I read in the Houston Chronicle the horrifying and disturbing details of his death. And when I heard our children scream and cry each night for their daddy on their tear-soaked pillows. And when I heard his mother and father weep for their firstborn son and for their grand-children. However, of all the torture I had experienced, nothing could prepare me for the trauma I endured when they lowered my husband's body six feet underground.

Even the words "survival guide" feel like they are lacking, because I know better than anyone that there is no step-by-step guide to survive this. I can only share my experience with the hope that it can be a light to fellow widows as they blindly crawl through this dark abyss. Don't be alarmed if you come across my makeshift tents in the abyss, I visited that place a lot.

After his funeral, I called several friends who were widowed in previous years in hopes of hearing some secret to navigating the pain, desperate for the slightest relief from the torment. I called my friend Lucy Hines often. Over time, as she listened to my sorrow, I became aware that there is no escape; that all who are grieving must endure the unrelenting, maddening nightmare of their own journey of grief *alone*. Although loved ones and mental health professionals will stand by your side when they can, you will soon find that there will be long stretches of solitude as you walk the trenches alone. The widow's journey of grief is lonely on many levels. We feel alone because we lost our soulmate, our best friend. We feel alone because life goes on for everyone else (even our own family must return to work and activities as usual). We feel alone in our community, no longer able to relate to humanity. We feel alone in life as we question our place within it.

Chapter 4

Survival Mode

My dearest love, my life is in upside-down disarray. The calls have stopped, and the visits from family and friends have dwindled to a rarity. As the new head of the household and leader of the family, I have no idea what I'm doing. I struggle to keep my head above water, trying to maintain our household, put three children under seven to bed, get them ready for school before 6:30 a.m., report to my job as a high school teacher by 7:10 a.m., pick up our kids after school, complete homework, make dinner, clean up dinner, have bath time, do the laundry, rock our children as they cry themselves to sleep, and wake up tomorrow and repeat.

My love, if you want me to make it through this, you're going to have to do something! I'm angry at having to do all of this alone! I'm exhausted from the unceasing grind day in and day out with no break. God help me survive this!

*I*t was on a foggy-brained morning in survival mode that I received a call from the kids' principal after dropping them off at school. He said, "Ms. Ortiz, I know you're going through a lot, but Tony arrived at school without shoes. I'm sorry, but children are still required to attend school with shoes." I couldn't believe my ears! How could Tony not have shoes on!? Then I remembered how, as a three-year-old, he went through a phase of taking off his shoes in the car because he wanted to stay with me. I embarrassingly stumbled over my words, choking back the tears, and told him I would be there as soon as possible. I cried all the way to our son's school, saying, "God, please help me." I crossed town through Houston traffic to get his shoes from home, then back through traffic to his school, and then back to work again.

As widows navigate these calamitous, uncharted waters alone, they are pressured to return to a "normal" routine. However, after returning to this "normal" routine, nothing submerges a widow faster than another obstacle in life. To this day, it amazes me how few people attempt to empathize with those struggling in survival mode.

Just imagine that you are shoulder-deep in the repugnance of a wasteland, and then someone unloads a dump truck full of more putrid, fermented decay on your head while you hear someone say, "I know you're going through a lot." There is nothing more painfully eye-opening to the bereaved than experiencing society's lack of understanding. The expression "life goes on" permeates the widow's workplace, church, community, and her children's schools.

What does survival mode for a widow look like to an outsider looking in? This is the best analogy I can give, which still pales in comparison to the widow's reality. Imagine you are walking out of your house when suddenly you are plucked from the air by a helicopter and dropped into the middle of a raging sea, treading over forty-foot waves, all with a fifty-pound weight tied around your ankle and no hope of rescue in sight. With every fiber of your being, you struggle to keep your head, and your children's heads, above water. Most people, including those widowed, cannot possibly understand how dramatically a widow's brain has been altered and fractured by losing their spouse. This analogy is still an inadequate comparison to the catastrophic reality of widowhood, which leaves many of us feeling astronomical levels of anxiety, fearful that the next wave will submerge us below the surface.

Although it is good to encourage our loved ones to seek to understand what life is like for a widow, it is impossible for them to do so. Even other widows cannot fully understand the depth of another widow's loss for various reasons. How their spouse died may be different. They may or may not have the same number of children. They may or may not have their family and friends' support. They may or may not have financial stability. They may or may not be able to continue to work. They may have to look for new work. They may have to move and sell their beloved home. They may or may not be knowledgeable about car and home maintenance or caring for children. The list goes on and on. The point is, just as it is irrational to compare grief, likewise, it is irrational to tell someone how to grieve. I distinctly remember thinking that unless their husband blew up in an explosion, leaving them at the age of twenty-nine with three children under age seven, no one could possibly understand.

Survival mode is the best way to describe the aftermath of death because anyone processing the gravity of immense loss will tell you that it's more like existing than living. It is taxing on the entire nervous system. Survival experts who study survival techniques say that when a person is in a survival situation, their mind and body will biochemically react to these extreme levels of stress with survival mechanisms such as appetite suppression. When humans respond to a fearful or traumatic situation, they instantly transition from a normal, routine mode to hypervigilance, survival mode, where the brain flips a switch to put more neurological energy toward survival. After all, our brains are designed to keep us alive. So widows in survival mode are living with a brain that is unceasingly working overtime to not only process the vast range of emotions of grief but also striving to maintain their day-to-day duties like grocery shopping, caring for sick children, taking children to appointments, taking off work for bank or social security appointments, paying taxes, maintaining the car, staying on top of household chores, and more. So much is expected of the widow. Not only does our brain feel it has been struck with a two-by-four at the news of our spouse's death, but now we are expected to keep our wounded head above water as we plan their funeral, pick out a casket and tombstone, write a eulogy, choose their flower arrangements, call banks, cancel payments, settle debts, call our children's school, and attend our children's extracurricular and church activities, all with a smile on our face. A widower is now Daddy *and* Mommy as he learns to take on duties as the primary caretaker and nurturer of the home. A widow is now Mommy *and* Daddy as she learns how to take on fatherly duties as the head of the household and disciplinarian. Even if the roles were swapped, the widow left behind is now flooded with their partner's role.

I will never forget the very first moment the shock began to subside ever so slightly and the veil was lifted just enough for me to grasp the reality of my life as a young widow. The truth is, there is nothing to prepare the widow for the depth of such pain and trauma.

Chapter 5

Triggers—Surviving Holidays, Weddings, Milestones, Family Events, and More

My dearest love, I sit here staring out the window, day-dreaming about how different our children would be if you had been given the chance to shape them, to love them, to teach them. I stare at the page of Daniella's chemistry homework—this cipher might as well be in Japanese kanji! She wants to be a doctor—this is your field! You were the genius chemistry and mathematics double-major! I can still picture us in my dorm room eating bologna sandwiches as we dreamed of our future, and can still hear you say, "I can't wait to help our kids with physics, trigonometry, and organic chemistry!" Yet, here I am, your substitute?

My love, how do I begin to describe the gaping holes in our hearts from all the deficits you didn't get to fill? We've needed you every day of these past nine years, and we will continue to feel the void of your loss in our hearts forever. We will always feel the immensity of losing you, the mourning from which is unending.

One thing I can promise you, my love, is this: on days that I feel defeated, I will show our babies that even a weary young widow can be the victor over pain and sorrow in my trying. With my will that surpasses all the obstacles thrown before me, I defiantly press onward. Just to get out of bed each day is progress. To say that there is still joy and sunshine to be felt in this life is progress. And though I may not seize the day, I am showing our children and showing myself how to love past the pain. In this way, I win! And just like you, love has saved me too.

Every widow struggles with triggers. It could be the sound of sirens, the smell of a cologne or perfume, the sound of gunshots, witnessing a wedding, or attending a funeral. My personal triggers, and the emotions they cause, are still difficult to discuss in detail to this day. For me, they include the sound of fire-engine sirens, the smell of smoke, Valentine's Day displays in stores, and funerals just to name a few. Especially in the beginning, there were times when it felt like my triggers knocked the wind out of me, and I would be on the verge of collapse. Something that is misunderstood is that triggers can be seemingly happy things. For me, it was attending football and baseball games and seeing dads carry their children on their shoulders, tossing the baseball to their children, and other activities. For widowers, it could be seeing a mother braid their daughter's hair, mothers and daughters wearing matching dresses, or even a commercial for feminine needs as dads wonder to themselves: "How on earth am I going to raise my daughter(s) without their mother?"

The truth is, surviving triggers was, and still is, very hard for me. What helped me personally survive big triggers, such as family holidays and important milestones, was when I expressed my anticipated pain beforehand. The evening before a close friend's wedding or my child's kindergarten graduation, I would sit in my closet and listen to our wedding song, read his love letters, or look at photos of him holding our babies or cheering me on during my C-section births. I would allow myself to feel all the pain, sadness, loneliness, and rage. I called it "having a good cry." For me, singing, writing, or even going for a five-mile run could not replace the healing relief of having a good cry. Although this may not help everyone, it helped me. Some may be afraid to start crying for fear they won't stop. Others may not know how to cry because it has been so long since they have. Or others may not get the same release from crying as they do from exercise, painting, dancing, or other things.

Chapter 6

Loss of Spouse, Loss of Identity, Loss of Friends & Family

My dearest love, before I even open my eyes, my head reels
in insufferable torture at the realization that my best friend,
my soulmate, and the father of my children is dead. Every
muscle in my body contorts and tightens, wrenched by the
pain. I reach my hand across the bed where you've slept
for the past nine years, once so warm from your presence
and now icy cold, and I feel the chill in my soul. I miss you
spooning me at night to warm me (or me spooning you so
I can cram my ice-cold toes behind your knees and laugh
when you scream, "Your toes are freezing!").

And now our friends are no longer calling. I have no
one. My stomach perpetually feels as though the ground

beneath me has vanished and I am free-falling into a dark abyss. With each waking day, the reality of your death hits me like a blow to the skull, leaving my head reeling in pain. While processing all of this, I contemplate that, if you're dead, then I am no longer a wife. If I am not your wife, then who am I? I am filled with terror of the obscure, dark, and cold unknown. I still cannot believe this is my life.

*W*idowhood is a massive tornado that fractures the mind, body, heart, and soul with not only the incomprehensible loss of your spouse but also the loss of your own identity. I vividly remember how I struggled to relate to others because I no longer knew who I was, much less what to say in a pleasant conversation.

When you lose your spouse, you are no longer a wife or husband, and no longer part of a normal family. Widows become the heads of their households, and widowers become the primary homemakers and caretakers of the children. Your spouse is no longer with you on the sidelines of your children's games, and no longer sitting next to you in the pew. Even more painfully felt is the sting when invitations from friends stop coming. Widows can develop an aversion toward their friendships, which have now become entangled with painful feelings of abandonment, neglect, and isolation.

People who have not suffered a traumatic event like this have a level of comfort due to their rational understanding of the world. The widow grieves this loss of comfort. Trauma has affected their ability to trust because their old life has been ripped away from them and their children. The widow must now go on living an alien existence with a foreign identity, an unknown future, and an unsure purpose. In short, the widow no longer understands the world the way everyone else still does, and this affects their identity. I remember saying to myself, "I once knew who I was and where I was going, but now I wonder who I am, where I'm going, and what to do."

My childhood and college friends remember me as quite the jokester. I was always up for the challenge to act or sing for a crowd to put a smile on my friends' faces. Many of my friends may remember a theater skit during our teen years when I played the role of Abraham who was to sacrifice his only son, Isaac, for God. While wearing a huge, round pillow stuffed underneath my shirt, I sent my sixteen-year-old, sprightly body sailing through space without restraint, launching myself across the stage onto another girl who was playing the ram. I held none of the true Julie back.

However, after my husband died, it felt as though the happy-go-lucky Julie died too. That once lively, jovial, magnetic soul was no more. The death of my husband fractured my mind and greatly altered my disposition to be more of a quiet, humble peacemaker for several years. My self-confidence withered and faded without his hugs and kisses, daily affirmations, and the love and support he showed as my best friend cheering me on in life. He believed in me like no one else did.

I now realize that mourning both the death of Javier *and* the death of Julie was a natural part of the grieving process. However, the real Julie still lay dormant below the surface. I noticed that the more steps toward healing I took, the more the real Julie would emerge through the many masks I wore. Just as a patient doesn't get back to work right after massive brain surgery, it takes time and care to heal the mind once it has been fractured by grief.

Losing our identity also causes us to dislike the stranger we become and yearn for the familiar person we once were. I used to try so desperately to get back to the happy-go-lucky Julie I once was. However, I realize now that both are Julie. Now I can say that I love my eight-year-old self, my eighteen-year-old self, my thirty-eight-year-old self, and one day I will say the same for my seventy-eight-year-old self and beyond! No one told me this. I had to learn to grieve the loss of the old me and accept the new me all on my own.

On days I felt low and self-loathing, I visualized telling my twenty-nine-year-old self: "Julie, we will never be the same person that we were before. Javier died, but we *will* learn to laugh again, we *will* learn to love life again, and we *will* learn to love ourselves again." I imagine she wouldn't believe me—no doubt she could never imagine laughing again—and would ask, "How could we?" I would tell her the words I journaled years ago: "Because you and Javier believed with all of your hearts that life's meaning is drawn from how deeply we love one another. This is the whole reason Javier fell in love with you in the first place—because of how beautifully you loved. Never give up on that. Never lose hope." Freely grieving the loss of my identity as Javier's wife has slowly given me a new understanding and love of myself.

The Loss of Friends & Family

The calamity of grief fractures your life in so many ways, causing rifts in many different directions, much like a lightning strike severs and splinters an oak tree, one of the strongest structures on this earth. Not only have you lost your soulmate and identity, now you are losing friends and family. The invitations to your friends' baby showers and children's birthday parties have stopped, all because you had tears in your eyes at the last child's party when you realized your husband will never light the candles on your child's cake again. Suddenly, you feel like a feather in the wind, completely unaware of where you are going, much less who you are. All you're doing is surviving. And I don't have to tell you that being in this constant, panicked state of survival takes a toll on you mentally, physically, and emotionally.

Nothing could prepare me for the loneliness that ensues after friends drift away. I felt frustrated and embarrassed when friends and coworkers were constantly filtering their words in fear that I would break. I remember wondering why they had stopped calling, why they had stopped inviting me. Those who are grieving may discover that many of their friends and family are no longer by their side for a plethora of reasons, and it is helpful to both the widowed person and their friend to get to the root of it by asking why this is happening.

Some friends may feel completely unaware of how to connect to the drastically altered widow who now stands before them. Some friends may be afraid of your traumatic situation (because nothing forces you to question your own mortality more than the death of a close friend). Some friends may distance themselves because they feel they're at a loss for words and don't want to say the wrong thing. Some friends may also feel threatened by their inadequacy to help you (especially when they compare themselves to those new friends in your grief support group who can relate to you on a level they cannot).

The widow may also subconsciously or inadvertently distance themselves from family and friends who say hurtful things, which they will discover is a hindrance in their grieving process. I remember the pressure that my friends unknowingly placed upon me to trust in God, to the point that I was afraid to express my true feelings of anger, resentment, loneliness, despair, and more. For example, a friend I loved very much went adrift when she told me (very soon after my husband's death), "If people are sad or depressed, it is because they don't trust God enough." Even though I knew intellectually that my faith would see me through this, emotionally and spiritually, I was struggling, and comments like hers were only making my burden doubly difficult and adding to my sorrow. Not to mention, there are a number of clichés widows hear, which are not conducive to healthy grieving. The whole, "It was his time" bit makes us feel sick. How can it be a thirty-year-old father's time?! The whole, "God needed another angel," or, "He's/She's in a better place." Sure, we may nod, smile, and hug you with a face soaked in tears because initially, we're in shock.

We accept your clichés, because what else can we do? However, after the shock wears off, we feel emotions—like rage, resentment, and bitterness—toward phrases like these. We understand that people want to help us to feel better and just don't know what to say, but we only hope to be crystal clear in our honesty about how these clichés truly make us feel. As I said in the Introduction, the best thing to say to comfort a widow is nothing! Even if you believe these clichés are true statements, you have no way of knowing where the grieving person is in their grief process, and you can do more harm than good with your words. (In fact, the grieving person may not even know where they are in their grief process.) The best way to help widows is by allowing them to be in the safety of your presence, to allow them to feel all that they need to feel, all while walking alongside them throughout the process. Quietly offer your shoulders to cry on, arms to hold them, and ears to listen to them.

In retrospect, I now realize that I had to distance myself from these friends and family in order to obtain the luxury and liberty of feeling my authentic feelings freely. If you are a friend of a widow or widower, you must understand that they will be greatly altered by this traumatic event, because not only have they lost their spouse, soulmate, and parent to their children, but they lost their identity too. What's equally difficult for a widowed person is coming to terms with the realization that the trauma they have endured has affected their ability to trust the world as they once knew it. Before their spouse's death, the suffering of this experience could only be imagined. But now that this painful nightmare has become their reality, they feel the ultimate, indescribable betrayal.

They may feel betrayed by their belief system, betrayed by the world, and betrayed by all that they once understood to be true. When they are in pain and afraid, they simply need friends with whom they can feel safe, speak freely, and be honest. Someone who is unafraid to be by their side as they go through the dark void, sometimes again and again. The word "compassion" is derived from the Latin meaning "suffer with." A friend who shows true compassion is willing to suffer with the widow or widower. Although it is uncomfortable for friends to wade through the mucky trenches with them, the unwavering support of these true friends is the ultimate expression of love. I recall the countless times I called my friends Elizabeth Martinez and Melisa Palermo as they sat with me and simply listened as I wept. As widows rebuild their identity and rediscover how to live life again, this is all they need—for friends to supportively stand by their side.

As you navigate the stages of grieving, you may also find yourself connecting with new friends who understand the pain and trauma and can emotionally support you on a deeper level. I have had many close friends walk with me through my journey of grieving, however, it doesn't compare to the way my friend David helped me through the trenches early on after my husband had died.

David was a helicopter pilot for the United States Army, and he had recently returned stateside after his Kiowa Warrior chopper tragically crashed during a mission in Afghanistan. As a result of the crash, he was paralyzed from the waist down. I reached out to David after a mutual friend (also a UST alumnus) said, "Did you hear President Obama visited David Ortiz in the hospital?" We had an instant connection. It was not only because we were enduring the most catastrophic events of our lives; it was also because our lives (as we knew them) had been irreparably shattered and we were both learning how to rebuild them without those indispensable pieces of ourselves. We were both struggling with our new reality and our new understanding of the world. How could my husband kiss me goodbye that morning and be dead before lunchtime? How could David go out, pilot his chopper the same way he had a hundred times before, and never walk again? How could two joyous young people (both still in their twenties) endure such calamitous, incalculable loss?

One day I told David that the trauma had so gravely altered my state of mind that I was now questioning *everything*. Life. The world. God. The metaphysical. The world had been transformed before my eyes from a warm, joyous place to a cold, merciless one. It was now a place I struggled to trust. It was a place I no longer understood the way "normal" people do. To be bombarded with an existential crisis on top of all the other emotions grief brought had left me feeling even more lost.

To hear the words, "I understand, Julie," was an immense relief, because I no longer felt alone. I had a friend by my side. We both soon learned that life as we knew it was lost forever. There was no going back. So we decided that our new mindset must be to adapt and learn how to live this new life that's been forced upon us. And, though we faced days where we were tempted to feel defeated, we never succumbed. We encouraged one another to have faith, keep moving forward, and never give up. That is what made our friendship so strong.

One distinct conversation with David that I will never forget was when I told him that I had tried swimming without using my legs in the deep end of the pool because I wanted to know better what it felt like to be in his situation. With all of my might and energy, I ferociously tried to dog paddle across the deep end using only my arms. After just a few minutes, I began to sink. The more I tried, the further I sank. I realized that it was impossible to swim without the use of my legs, and my heart sank. I swam to the side of the pool and sobbed. I could not fathom what it would be like to never use my legs again. The terror that gripped me was only imagined, but David had to live a lifetime with this tremendous burden that would affect him every day for the rest of his life.

After hopelessly trying to swim without my legs, I also realized that no one could see the invisible wounds that David bore, just as no one could fathom my invisible wounds from losing my soulmate, the father of my children, my identity, many of my friends, and even my understanding of the world. Though we could never compare our losses, nor the unique profundity of our sorrow, for each of us to have a friend that was unafraid to enter the abyss with us was a gift beyond measure.

I share the impact that David's friendship had on my life to demonstrate that the friends who have remained the closest to me are those who could simply be with me as I treaded the turbulent waters of grief. They did not tell me how to "feel better," nor did they tell me what to do, where to go, or how to think. They were simply with me and loved me through it all, and I was with them and loved them through it all. The presence of these few steadfast friends who helped me weather the storm reaffirmed my faith in God's providential love. I now see with such clarity that God sends us people during different seasons to help us weather life's darkest tempestuous storms, just as God sends us to help others in their hour of need. He sends friends who encourage us, like when I told David I'm going to write a book and he responded, "Crush it, Julie!"

Now wiser for the wear, I embrace both the steadfast friendships before my husband's death, and the newfound friendships gifted to me after his death. I also see that questioning doesn't ever go away, no matter how old we get. Fatimah Asghar said, "Every year I manage to live on earth, I collect more questions than answers." Although I will never understand why life can be so cruel, I am grateful for its blessings.

It would have helped me as a young widow to read this book and learn that it's okay to tell my friends specifically what it is I need by saying, "*All* I need is for you to sit with me and listen." Who are the people in your life who can offer nurturing, kind, or practical support? We cannot choose the families we are born into. If the only family and friends you have exhibit toxic behaviors, is it possible for them to offer practical assistance at arm's length? This means you will have to establish boundaries and stand by those boundaries (especially when your children are involved). If you have no one, are there grief support groups in your community or faith community? Some practical examples of how others can help include cooking meals, mowing the lawn, servicing the car, grocery shopping, house cleaning, home maintenance, childcare, finding a good counselor, or other things. Some examples of nurturing activities could be sitting and talking with a friend, visiting the cemetery, going to church or a therapy group together, or making therapeutic crafts together (painting, pottery, gardening, visiting nature).

I'm not sure I even noticed everyone who came to stay with me or show support since much of the time immediately following my husband's death is a hazy blur. Initially, I recall that I spent many days walking around the house with blood-shot eyes in a state of panic, utter shock, and denial. I will never stop asking God to bless all the people who helped my children and me in the wake of this catastrophe.

SECTION 2:
Self-Care Physically

Chapter 7

Basic Care of Our Body

I know what you're thinking—it seems so silly and obvious to even mention, right? Why is there an entire chapter on this? I practically heard you scoff from here! I know I scoffed when counselors handed me pamphlets that spoke about depression and maintaining self-care: feeding myself daily, showering, combing my hair, changing my day-three pajamas—sniff, sniff—correction, day-seven pajamas.

Well, there's an entire chapter dedicated to this because it's commonly avoided until a domino-effect cascades the widow or widower into a muddled mess, unable to move or even care about their present state of *dire* need. This is real talk. I know what it feels like to be completely physically spent. To smell your own underarms in disbelief that it's even possible for such a pretty woman to smell this bad! I felt grotesque as I hobbled over to the kitchen for morsels and scraps of food and then slithered back to the TV, stroking it like Gollum from *Lord of the Rings* as he whispers, "My precious!" I know the feeling of bartering with yourself: "Well, I only have time to either eat or shower before work, so I guess I'm going to starve this morning." And I know what it's like to try to rationalize with yourself when you are not eating properly by saying, "Well, I ate a sliver of toast this morning, so at least I ate today." These are things I would actually tell myself. I would rather veg out on the couch, distracted from the pain by my precious TV, than expend the energy to take a shower.

To put it bluntly, if we do not take care of our bodies, we are not being our best selves for our children. I didn't believe this at first. Yet here I am, nine years later, as my kids and I sit recovering from strep throat, and I feel like I'm not even practicing what I preach because it's so hard for us solo moms and dads to prioritize self-care when our kids have extra needs. Solo moms and dads are the first to tell you that they come last, however, this is a dangerous way to live and will always end in ruin because we are people, not robots. If I am empty, I have nothing to give. I learned as a young widow that we must learn to care for ourselves first. For some widows, this may come easily. For other widows who struggle with self-love, it may not come so naturally (especially if they have suffered from past traumas, which is discussed in Section 3). Trust me, the work of a solo mom is unending, but we must care for ourselves in order to care for others. Even though it seems so basic, it is so often neglected.

Chapter 8
I'm a Sluggish Insomniac!

While in survival mode, there are some widows who hit the gym and can't wait to exert all of their energy. They can seem so perfect! I asked one of my widower friends from my support group how he found the energy and stamina to hit the gym with all of the exhaustion we face from single-parenting while grieving. He told me that he slept better if he exhausted himself physically. For him, he noticed that if he didn't exert his frustrations, anxieties, and pain in physical exercise, then he would suffer from insomnia all night long. The first thing that popped into my head was, wow! I guess I'm a sluggish insomniac! I don't have the determination. The second thing I thought was, how is someone this in-tune with their body that they can practically hear what their body is telling them? Do I have this too and I'm just ignoring it?

The answer is yes! That's because our bodies are designed to be pushed to the max. Just when we feel our tank is on empty, we push ourselves harder. My Dad pointed out how obvious this is when you look at a marathon runner who is completely out of gas and collapses, yet musters up the energy to still crawl across the finish line even though his legs have stopped working. Like all widows, I was pushing my body to the max and was completely unaware of the warning signs my body was screaming out because I had not yet developed that part of myself. In time, I discovered the word "self-awareness," which is the first step toward changing behaviors and working toward a better quality of life.

The fact is, *we can't heal what we don't know is sick*. Have you ever noticed that when you're in a survival situation, adrenaline can mask the pain from an injury? One day I was hiking in the woods, and a swarm of bees appeared around me. My adrenaline kicked in, sending me running over logs and fallen branches. Unbeknownst to me, I got cuts and bruises all over my knees and legs. I didn't even notice until much later when the adrenaline had worn off. Similarly, when a widowed person is in survival mode and simply trying to put one foot in front of the other, he or she is completely unaware of the numbed pain they are in.

Please keep in mind that the widower who told me of his fitness success may have been further along in his grieving process than I was, and it is always nonsensical to compare ourselves to others (something else I learned). Comparing grief or personal healing will only stunt healing and cause more suffering. Grief is grief. Pain is pain. It does no one any good to try to decipher who has it worse. Comparison is the thief of joy. Let us celebrate our own healing just as much as the healing of others.

The importance of this section is to learn the value of taking steps (even if they're the tiniest steps) toward healthy coping during this grieving process. I understand the vicious cycle that tempts us to compare ourselves and then feel guilty about ourselves when we're stuck. My hope is to help other widows to understand that when we continue to avoid our basic needs, we will be like the exhausted marathon runner who starts to break down. All we can do is try our best and take one step at a time. Some days we will succeed, others maybe not, but we are still trying.

As I end this chapter, I am so proud of myself for doing just that! I went to the gym, began the tough sport of pow-erlifting (I was the only female in my lifting group), and by the end of the year, I reached my goal of lifting more than my husband's body weight (and more than double my own body weight)! After I deadlifted two-hundred-sixty-five pounds, my Dad asked me how I was able to achieve such a goal. I told him that each time I lifted the barbell, I imagined I was lifting my precious Javier out of the flames of the inferno and carrying his body to safety. Widows are some of the strongest human beings on the planet!

Chapter 9

Humans are Social Creatures

My dearest love, how can I describe the soothing power of your touch? I still remember the way you would run into the room and tickle me! I would roar in laughter at the sight of you wiggling your "tickle fingers" before you even touched me! I remember seeing your eyes light up with the most beautiful smile as we laughed and played. These memories are bittersweet. Remembering the way you held my hand in church or caressed my head as I faded off to sleep makes my heart ache. Your touch was always a healing balm to my soul—what power you had to instantly soothe me physically, psychologically, emotionally, and mentally. I recall how I would put my head on your chest as you stroked my head so softly, and the way you put your hand on the small of my back when leading me into a crowded room, showing me you always had my back. And, forgive me for saying, but the way you came up behind me acting like a Catholic rabbit when I bent over to pick up the kid's toys off the floor! Also, the way you kissed the tears off my cheeks over and over again, thanking me for our babies' C-section deliveries as you witnessed doctors put my organs back and staple me shut. And the inseparable joining of our bodies and souls during the passion of our marital love—so ground-shaking that I swear the heavens opened up—and then to look at the little faces our love made. My Javier, all of your little expressions of love in the millions of times we touched during your life is enough to fill a million lifetimes! Thank you for choosing me.

Humans are social creatures. It is often forgotten how important human contact is. We wilt when we don't have physical touch from our loved ones. When we are present and connecting with another human being, we are giving to both ourselves and others. For this reason, wholesome health is often written about in three categories: caring for ourselves physically, mentally, and emotionally. This is because humans are body, mind, and spirit. It is vital to our entire being to be healthy in each way. A healthy body supports a healthy mind, which supports a healthy spirit, and vice versa. If your body is unwell, your mind won't be any different.

Online interaction cannot replace in-person socialization. This is understood now more than ever. During the global pandemic, all people have felt the emotional pain and mental strain of isolation, and it's also obvious that online contact is nowhere near close to meeting our needs for this physical and emotional contact. Humans need to physically come in contact with one another, whether it be a warm embrace, holding hands, rough-housing with the kids, reading bedtime stories, or even just looking into a loved one's eyes during conversation.

Although it's common for adults to forget how important this is, it often comes naturally to children to cope with discomfort through play. There's a reason therapists recommend play therapy when processing our grief. It is through this innate, basic expression of ourselves that our grief is felt and healing ensues. So express your sorrow and pain in playing with your children, your nieces/nephews, your students, your siblings, or your friends.

Each of my siblings helped me regain my playful spirit in their own way. I often played with my youngest sister, Michelle, when we visited my dad and spent the night. We would stay up late talking in a British accent, playing poker until we got that royal flush, swimming in the local pool screaming, "Oh gosh, I drank the water!" after some kid said they peed, and once even wrote over one hundred words for the john because we were *that* bored! Play is so important to healing.

SECTION 3:
Self-Care Mentally

Chapter 10

Helping Our Children Grieve

My dearest love, my legs are covered with black and blue bruises from Tony spontaneously walking up and biting down on my legs as hard as he possibly can, to the point that I have to pry his jaws from my thigh. He's so angry! Angry at me for "disappearing in my mind" as I constantly space out. I'm lost in my grief with incessant racing thoughts of all I need to do with work, finances, home maintenance, caring for the children, and the list goes on and on.

Despite trying my hardest to play Legos with the boys today, as we sat together zooming the little cars on the floor, Gabriel suddenly looked up at me with his big, precious eyes and asked, "Mommy, when is Daddy coming home?" And then he paused before remembering, "Oh yeah, I forgot, Daddy's dead. He's in Heaven now . . .

Mommy, when can I go to Heaven?" It took the breath right out of me. I must've looked as pale as a ghost in that moment as the life drained from my body at his innocent request. I couldn't even find the words, much less the strength, to respond to our sweet boy. I had to get up, walk away, and cry so deeply from the depths of my withered soul until my entire body ached with fatigue. When I finally lost the strength to keep sobbing, I returned to play cars and Gabe responded, "It's okay, Mommy, I'm done with playing cars," as if he didn't want to bother me because he could feel how sad I was.

Our babies should not be trying to take care of their mother! I feel as if they have lost both of their parents in many ways. It isn't fair! We're going to need more help than just counseling once a week. We all need more. They need their mom back.

Widows with children are some of the strongest people on the planet, whether we want to be or not. We are doubly burdened with processing our own grief while simultaneously helping our children process theirs. And this applies to children of all ages. Every widow knows how drastically their children's lives are altered.

Whether they're two weeks old or twenty years old, they still grieve, and their lives are still affected by this trauma. And not just because they lost a parent, but because, in many ways, they have lost *two*. The parent who is left behind is lost, walking around as a shell of a person in survival mode. Undoubtedly they are doing their best to stay the same person they were, but it's important to understand that even the strongest human beings are altered by trauma.

The widow with children is facing the unimaginable: caring for the daily needs of their children and helping them to grieve, all while attempting to process their own grief. To understand a glimpse of what it's like for the grieving widow to help their children to grieve, just imagine you are dropped into the sea, treading above forty-foot waves, all with a fifty-pound weight tied around your ankle and no help in sight. Then someone hands you a child . . . or two . . . or three . . . or four. Soon after my husband's death, I tried to "return to normal" by taking my little children, aged three, five, and seven, to the movie theater. Like most children's movies, one of the characters died in a tragic accident. As I witnessed this tragic death on the big screen, I couldn't hold my pain in any longer. I began to sob in a theater full of people and ran out to cry in the hallway for a few minutes. I remember thinking that I wished I could escape my pain and remain unfazed the way my children *seemed* to be. However, after leaving the cinema, my daughter said, "Mommy, it's so sad how he died just like Daddy did." I was wrong. They felt it too. The little grieving hearts and minds of children are trying to cope with their sorrow just as much as adults.

It is a common pitfall for widows to neglect themselves, however, this directly affects their children's grieving process.

The most important piece of advice that I wish someone had told me is that now, more than ever, is the time to accept help for the sake of your children. Have you ever noticed how a flight attendant demonstrates that the first step to staying alive in a survival scenario is for the parent to put on their *own* oxygen mask first before helping their children? Why? It is not because we care about ourselves more than our children; it is because we cannot take care of anyone else if we are not alive. If widows don't care for themselves, they will have nothing left to give. In short, if widows are not well and healthy, their children will suffer for it. I have noticed over the years that when widows are caring for their own physical, mental, and spiritual health to the best of their ability, their children are ultimately cared for as well.

I distinctly remember going to a meeting at the Social Security office with my dad when I hadn't eaten anything that day (and maybe even the day before). My brain had suppressed my appetite in this survival situation to the point that I never even felt hungry. In fact, each time I thought of my husband, his accident, or the nightmare of my life, I would feel nauseous and unable to eat. As a result, when I got out of my car, everything went black and the sounds in the parking lot faded. I nearly hit the pavement as my body flopped back into the driver's seat. I gave myself a couple of minutes to just breathe. As I waited for the blood to return to my face, I told myself, "Thank God I didn't faint in front of my children. I really need to take better care of myself." I dug around the children's car seats, found some old snacks, and said, "I guess this is breakfast!" On days when the nausea was really bad, I would force myself to drink protein shakes, which really seemed to help sustain me.

Another struggle widows endure is insomnia. Having gone days and weeks without sufficient sleep, it became impossible for me to function properly and resulted in "widow's brain fog." After consecutive days in this state, I would forget my phone or purse at home when I went to the store, get stranded after locking my keys in my car, or get lost on a busy freeway because I forgot where I was going. Every widow will have dozens of stories like this. The widow in survival mode must eventually realize that it's okay to accept help.

In addition to processing our own grief in counseling, our children likewise need counseling. As our children's sole caretaker, we need to advocate for them getting care and help to process their grief. Many adults often forget that children have little minds in need of healing therapy too. Depending on their age, this might mean sitting down with a counselor and sharing how they feel. Children are commonly referred to play therapy, where they express their grief in various mediums. Play therapy includes anything from finger-painting, working with clay, dancing, rock-painting, interacting with animals, and ordinary playing.

After the funeral, my family told me about Bo's Place, a free grief program here in Houston for parents and children. Bo's Place had a therapy group for adults in one space and a separate, age-appropriate space for play therapy for the children. They even planted a flower for Daddy in the garden there. This experience was so healing and helpful for my children and me that we went many times. They expressed their emotions in so many different ways among other children who had also lost a parent. It was an immense comfort to myself and my children to hear other children comfort each other with empathy and understanding. After my children told their classmates in school that their daddy died in an explosion, they soon learned not to tell their friends. The reactions they received made them feel as though they had the plague. However, when my children told their friends in their play therapy group, they casually responded, "Yeah, my mommy died of a brain tumor. She's in Heaven too. Let's go play!" The relief your children receive in learning they are not alone in the world is a true comfort to them.

My children's school counselor was also very helpful by offering ways for them to cope while in school and a safe place for them to freely share their grief. My family also helped me search for therapy options in my area and helped me find the best fit. In your case, you may have to ask several mental health facilities, community centers, and churches about what programs are available. And don't be afraid to ask about free sessions or sliding-scale payment options.

I also want to briefly discuss children with unique, special, and/or medical needs. As a mother of children with various needs, such as ADHD, dyslexia, and even incurable diseases like type 1 diabetes which demand extra care, I understand more than anyone how overwhelming and insufferable life can feel. Throughout the years when serious illnesses and learning disabilities emerged, I grieved the loss of my husband all over again. I needed my husband, my best friend. The children needed their father. There is nothing worse than receiving a diagnosis that your child has a learning disability or serious illness and bearing this life-altering news *alone*. No one would care as much as he would. I know every widow reading this understands.

Despite the burden of grief weighing heavily upon us, sometimes life has a way of heaping more struggles upon us. Even small obstacles can make us feel overwhelmed. It's as if life says, "You survived that forty-foot wave! Take a breath, because here comes an eighty-foot wave!" Not to mention the pressure to bear it all as a champion with a smile, always masking our pain and anxiety.

One day, I received a call from my child's principal just a few days before the one-year memorial of my husband's death. I had already been grieving because I felt the change of the weather in my bones, which caused my body to grieve before my mind realized it. The principal, teachers, and learning specialists broke the news to me that my brilliant child had been diagnosed with ADHD, dyslexia, and Irlen syndrome. They proceeded to convey their sympathies for my husband's death, but there were no words of solace to be had that day. Though my eyes began to well up with tears, I suppressed my feelings so that I could be what my child needed me to be. The gravity of hearing such news is indescribable. It plunged me back into the abyss where the leaden emotions of grief came flooding back, pushing me under all over again. During these overwhelmingly difficult moments of bearing bad news when I nearly felt my knees shake and buckle beneath me, I would take deep breaths to reset my nervous system, say a prayer for God to help carry me through, and ask Javier to be with his children and me.

These are the most difficult moments for parents as we place our grief aside, muster up the strength to be present, be what our child needs us to be, and rise to the challenge that lay before us. And it may be especially difficult if we felt we had been making progress in our grieving process, only to now be cast into the sea of despair once again. All I can share with you is that each obstacle life placed in my path prompted me to learn and grow as a mother, solo parent, and leader of the family as I became my children's most invaluable advocate.

There is no better human being on the face of this earth for this job than *you*! *You* are the one to ensure that your child's entire being is cared for: body, mind, and spirit. *You* are the one who will advocate for your child's unique needs and his/her care at this fragile time, whether that be in the classroom, at home, or through medical or mental health care. *You* are now the person to effect the biggest change in the course of their lives, which ultimately affects your life too. Of all the people I have encountered in this journey, widowers and widows who parent children with special needs are truly superheroes in my book!

Chapter 11
Visiting Their Grave

My dearest love, our Dani, Gabe, and Tony so beautifully expressed their grief in the pictures they drew of "Daddy together with us in Heaven." They asked me if you could leave Heaven to visit us on earth. Their faces dropped when I told them no. They want to see you so badly that they drew themselves in Heaven with you.

We placed many precious treasures in front of your tomb-stone as we shared the stories of your life in front of your grave. Gabriel shared the story of the time you put a Spi-derman mask on him and threw him from wall to wall. Tears flowed from our cheeks as he described how he cast his web, zipping through the house, swinging from wall to wall. My love, I will never forget how happy you made him feel. To him, he really was Spiderman!

Dani shared the story of how you effortlessly carried her on your shoulders at the Astros games and theme parks so she could see above everyone in the crowds. And we all laughed when she shared the song you invented on your guitar: "Dreadlock Horse!"

Tony shared the memory of your mouth-watering barbeque and freshly baked pies. And his face lit up in laughter as he shared the memory of you throwing him into a giant pile of fresh laundry as you both danced around the living room to your loud rock music.

I shared the story of our second missionary trip in Monterrey, Mexico, and how you picked up the children and zipped them through the air like airplanes while making sound effects. You were completely unphased by the lack of cleanliness around us from the lack of running water, poor waste and sewage systems, and inadequate housing. I also remembered when I first bore witness to the depth of your love and my heart whispered, "I'm going to marry that man!"

As we recounted these memories, we could no longer compose ourselves, and we all wept together, hugging each other firmly and holding one another up. When those who are left behind share their stories about you, I notice one thing in common: as they talk about you, they have shining eyes. All of them! Their faces are aglow at the mere utter-

ance of your name because of the way that you made them feel: loved. Your life was a life of sacrifice, selflessness, and faithfulness. Your life was a life of love.

For me, one of my favorite ways to grieve is to visit my husband's grave. It is an entire sacred ritual that is felt even in the days leading up to visiting him. The children and I bring him letters, art, gifts, flowers, or even poems and songs. We are often joined by family who share stories of him with our children. There may be many widows who can relate or many who disagree, but for me, though the cemetery is a place of mourning and tears, it is also a place of rest, solace, comfort, and peace; a place where I have cried from the depths of my being in indescribable sorrow and a place where I have wept with joy at the privilege of having shared my life with my beloved.

Chapter 12

Avoidance– Distraction from Pain

My dearest love, the counselor handed me another pamphlet on the stages of grief. Give me a break! Even though I know the importance of mental health from studying psychology, I always toss the pamphlets in the passenger seat of my minivan after therapy (where you used to sit when I drove), as if to say, "You deal with this, because I'm done with all this grief crap!" After all, isn't that what we did during our marriage when one of us needed a break? We would simply read one another's face of worry, exhaustion, despair, or sadness, and the other would step up and say, "No worries, baby, I've got you!" So out of rebellion toward the grief, I'm tossing these pamphlets to the side along with a stack of unchecked mail—signatures required—report cards for the kids, and my breakfast bagel that I forgot to eat, which is now as stale and dried up as my brain from all my racing thoughts! It's your turn to help with all this, and quite frankly, I'm so done with the whole rigmarole of grief! I'm done with "processing my feelings!"

*W*e widows are experts at denial and avoidance. I mean, as long as we're distracted from the pain, we can't feel it, right? So we teeter-totter between acceptance and denial. To accept, or not to accept—that is the widow's question. Quite bluntly put, we quickly learn to become masters at avoiding the pain of our reality.

But why? Why do we distract? Why do we avoid? Well, because distraction is a coping mechanism. It is instinctual for all human beings to avoid pain and seek comfort. Whether you realize it or not, you have been developing coping mechanisms like distraction to deal with pain and discomfort since you were an infant. During childhood, we develop these coping mechanisms to ease our maxed-out nervous systems and exhausted psyches. As children, there is an innate desire within us to distract ourselves and cope with the pain and discomforts of this world. We find ways to cope in playing with G.I. Joes and dolls, creating art, crying and kicking, playing sports, running on the playground, watching TV, and playing video games.

As we grew from children into adulthood, we adopted new coping mechanisms from learned behaviors in our environment. These learned coping mechanisms can range from overworking in the gym or eating a bunch of brownies to more harmful habits like alcoholism and substance abuse. Whether we realize it or not, turning to these coping mechanisms forms us into the person we are as a whole. Whether the widow's denial is perceived or not, the habit of turning to these coping mechanisms to help our bodies and minds cope with pain forms us into the people we are as a whole. Perhaps widows fall into these cyclical patterns or behaviors as a sort of "auto-pilot" mode while attempting to cope with their day-to-day important tasks. As they "go through the motions" of their daily routines they may not even be mindful of how destructive their compulsive self-medicating is becoming. When loving those who struggle with addiction, a spirit of mindfulness and understanding to help remove shame and focus on harm reduction is what is most needed by those in pain.

For example, when I was in high school, it felt euphoric to score a goal in soccer or sing for my congregation, both of which are healthy coping mechanisms. However, I also unknowingly developed harmful coping mechanisms like stress-eating a pint of ice cream at study groups while anxiously studying for midterms. Once I had discovered the wonderful world of Ben and Jerry's ice cream from college friends, it was hard to break the habit of self-soothing with comfort food. Changing your behavior is tough. It took self-awareness, time, and a lot of diligence and willpower to remember (and actually put into practice) the fact that

I love the way singing makes me feel more than harmful coping behaviors.

In this modern era, there is a plenitude of healthy and unhealthy coping mechanisms that grieving people use or misuse to self-soothe their unabating pain. To understand the widow's desperate need for relief, we must first strive to understand that the mind of the widow has been violently violated by trauma. This trauma initiates a domino effect of physiological reactions as the body's systems immediately shift into overdrive to protect the person. Although professionals and specialists can tell you more about the effects of trauma, a brief explanation is that our nervous system responds with a variety of reactions, including irregular breathing patterns, increased or decreased heart rate, inability to sleep, and sky-rocketing levels of stress hormones that directly affect the gut, causing symptoms like nausea, stomach cramping, and appetite suppression. Many of these physiological reactions within the body affect major systems like the heart and brain. It is often forgotten how much the chemistry of the brain affects other body systems. In short, psychological trauma directly affects physical health.

After days, weeks, and months of the entire body's systems being overworked and unmaintained, it begins to sputter. Using the analogy of a car, the check-engine light suddenly comes on, and we put our brains on cruise control, cruising through our days on auto-pilot. If we fail to heed the warning lights when our body alerts us that it needs sleep, nourishment, mental health, safety, or something else, then things will begin to break down and fall apart. This seems so basic when caring for our cars, but we often forget that if we fail to fuel up and maintain our bodies, they will break down too.

After a prolonged time coasting in survival mode, the widow will begin to seek relief through coping mechanisms (whether healthy or unhealthy) to rest the body's systems that are now completely spent. Examples of healthy distractions could be something as simple as watching TV or plugging into social media. However, these healthy distractions can become unhealthy if the person is avoiding feeling altogether. Whether it's staying continually glued to screens, becoming a workaholic, or overly exercising, the bottom line is that distractions should not be used to *perpetually* numb pain and prevent the widow from feeling anything.

One day my dad had to walk over to me and lovingly say, "Julie, it's time to sit down and rest." But I didn't know how. I looked like an anxiety-riddled Energizer Bunny who kept going and going, never allowing myself time to sit still so I wouldn't have to feel the pain. I was ceaselessly zipping around cleaning, shopping, and doing anything to stay busy and keep a full schedule.

Examples of unhealthy distractions can look like seeking chemicals from the outside, namely, alcohol and drugs, to attempt to balance the chemistry on the inside and assist our brains with numbing the pain. It can also look like misusing physical intimacy for temporary pleasure, eating disorders, self-harm, and a host of other things. Whether the widow uses unhealthy distractions or misuses healthy ones, one thing remains true: the widow is desperately hoping the pain, lone-liness, anxiety, and depression will subside.

Many widows who are several years in will tell you that there is a fine line between perpetual distraction and healthy distraction. What does healthy distraction look like? Well, it can look like what I am doing right now: writing. Coping with grief is learning to balance healthy coping mechanisms as we work through the stages of grief. Later in the book, I discuss healing through creativity, whether it's via the arts, physical fitness, or the sciences.

Chapter 13
Bad Habits Change Us

One of the most impactful things I have learned from attending grief support groups over the years is how using healthy or unhealthy distractions to avoid feeling emotions altogether (whether consciously or unconsciously) not only inhibits the grief process but can also instill bad habits. These bad habits, or vices, are not only difficult to stop once they're ingrained in us, but they can also change us over time into someone we do not want to be. Loving mothers and fathers who were once warm and kind can become bitter, callous, and distant. The pain, rage, and despair can ultimately morph them into strangers to all who know them.

What's more, the widow may say, "I don't care that I'm callous and distant, because if my husband/wife hadn't died, then I wouldn't have to be like this!" Once the widow feels that their behavior is not their fault (that instead, it's God's fault, the world's fault, or someone else's fault), then they slip further into unhealthy habits and further away from who they truly are. Even if it's illogical, some widows even blame their spouses for dying. I have heard widows angry at their spouses for dying of heart attacks, diseases, and even accidents. At one point, I felt angry at my husband for dying when I needed him to help me with things that only he could do, and I resented now having to learn to do those things on top of everything else.

It is important for me to tell you that although you will hear me say many times that the greatest gift we can give our children is our own healthy mental state, I do *not* want these words to sound preachy. I very clearly remember how angry I felt toward mental health professionals and pastors who made me inadvertently feel bad or guilty. Why do we widows feel this way? Well, it's just like when I wrote Javier that I was "done with this whole grief thing!" We're done with being labeled a widow! We're done with looking single (which is why we still wear our wedding ring, leave their hat on the dashboard, or leave their boots on the porch for *years*). We're done with looking like a single parent. We're done with walking into a crowded room and the tone changing because everyone's trying not to say the wrong thing and offend us. We just want to be normal again like everyone else! We want things to feel as comfortable and familiar as they used to, and the avoidance of our current reality is just plain easier than confronting our new circumstances. Not to mention the obvious, that processing grief is immensely, vastly exhausting.

Honestly, just thinking of my initial personal healing work is giving me a wicked migraine as I try to push past it and get these words out on paper. I remember how after difficult therapy sessions of releasing my pain, I would walk away so mentally and physically fatigued that I felt like I would blow over with a strong breeze. I understand how difficult it is to work through the pain. I also know that it was the right thing to do. During each therapy session, I felt a little healthier. Even if I didn't realize it that day, I came to realize it eventually. It is completely, one-hundred-percent true that on the days I stopped avoiding my pain and worked through my grief by allowing myself to feel my emotions, I was a better mother, daughter, sister, friend, and teacher.

The last thing you need is someone else telling you *how* to grieve when you may not currently have the energy to work on your grief. All I can do is offer my experience of my own personal survival during my grief process. One of the most fruitful things I did for myself was to write a list of balanced, interchangeable resources and healthy coping mechanisms and to simply choose from that list as needed:

- Spirituality: Prayer and meditation in words, songs, art, writing, church, liturgy, and more

- Play: My children, students, nieces, nephews, friends, and others.

- Human Connection: Family and friends (Adult interaction is important for widows and widowers with children. We are often starved of meaningful adult interaction)

- Community: Neighborhood, religious community, cultural community, sports community

- Therapy: Counseling, therapy with my children, play therapy

- Creativity: Art, drawing, painting, pottery, crafting, writing, or digital art

- Music: Singing, playing an instrument, performing for an audience, karaoke, and more

- Exercise: Sports like powerlifting, rock climbing, cycling, running, soccer, and others (Running and weightlifting were the best therapy for me.)

- Health: Nutritious food

- Nature: Being enveloped in mother nature, whether by taking a hike, swimming in the ocean, or some other activity

Due to the fog of grief, I spent a lot of time avoiding my talents by forming bad habits until I finally shook off the stranger I had become to find the real Julie below the surface. I was brought to my knees over and over again in the midst of the chaos and said, "God, there has to be a better way. You are that way." The ups and downs on this grief roller-coaster have taught me to turn to God, refocus my mind and heart, choose something on the list, and express my grief while doing it.

The main thing I want you to hear is this: grieving is a process unique to each and every person. Whether it be in a therapy session, grief-journaling, jogging, or helping our children grieve, we are allowing our hearts to actively express our joys and sorrows. Over the past nine years, I have discovered some of the most beautiful expressions of my grief in my songwriting, singing, writing, teaching, and above all, in loving my children.

Remember, grief is not a clear, charted path to healing. It is an obscure labyrinth with twists and turns that leave us feeling lost. What's more, we feel defeated and discouraged when our progress is halted and we find ourselves right back to square one. For example, I felt I had worked through the forgiveness stage, but then a year after the explosion on his memorial day, I was right back to feeling anger and resentment. Rest assured, any grief work is progress, even if it's just taking a much-needed nap. So even if it feels like two steps forward and five leaps back, be proud of yourself. Grief work is by far the hardest work you will ever do in your entire life.

With the grieving process also comes a wide range of experiences, from mountain-top highs to dark-valley lows. One minute you feel you're on top of the world, at the highest peak and ready to live life to the fullest, and the next minute you feel triggered and brought down to the dark valley. Triggers cause physiological and emotional trauma responses that can stop you in your tracks and can cause a profusion of emotions. Some of the physical responses can include an increased heart rate, increased or decreased breathing, and nausea from the release of cortisol. Some of the emotional responses can include panic, anxiety, rage, fear, despair, guilt, or loneliness. In short, triggers can affect the grieving person's entire central nervous system. These triggers resurrect the trauma the grieving person has suffered and leave them feeling utterly exhausted and drained after experiencing the roller-coaster of physiological and emotional strain.

I will share a story of how I felt I could conquer the world one minute, and felt leveled by a trigger the next. I was feeling on top of the world following a vacation where I had driven the children to Colorado through the snow and scheduled adventures like visiting the wolf conservation, ice fishing, and horse-sled riding. I told our babies, "We are going to do all the adventures Daddy wishes he could do but can't since he's in Heaven. We will do them for him, and in so doing, honor him by accomplishing our dreams!"

Soon after the trip, I went to the store to restock, and as I walked through the grocery store aisles, I subconsciously avoided the Valentine's Day display with a cornucopia of hearts, bears, and chocolates. Once I got to the front of the store, though, I approached yet another display, and I felt a wave had submerged me underwater once again. My entire body tightened with anxiety, my breath escaped my lungs, my brain had to remind my lungs to continue breathing, my stomach was sick with nausea, and my heart raced. I not only recalled that on each Valentine's Day he surprised me with special deliveries, but the lucid memory of the delivery he ordered while he was still alive and which Daniella and I received days after his death came flooding back. It took all of my strength to bottle up my feelings of pain, loneliness, despair, and rage that his love had been stolen from me. I even felt fury toward the store for displaying this mountain of pain! I checked out at the store and continuously asked myself on the walk to the car: Julie, what's wrong with you? You were doing so well! I thought you were past this!

Soon after this, my sister asked me, "Julie, how did you survive it? I could never imagine my husband and the father of my child dying." At the time, I was in a good place, as I responded, "I am just grateful to God for the gift of his love, and I'm trying to live every day to the fullest in his honor." Yet, here I was, feeling angry, alone, and like no one understood how I felt as I resented life and all within it! What's more, after regressing to the valley, I felt afraid to tell others my true, authentic feelings. I didn't want to disappoint them since I had recently told them how much "better" I was.

In retrospect, I now see the real answer to this question is: "I can't answer that question because I'm not done yet. I'm still surviving it." The truth is, I will grieve the loss of Javier for the rest of my life. And all those who loved him deeply will grieve him deeply for the rest of their life too.

We widows are constantly feeling guilty for our emotional mood swings and are constantly trying to "heal" to meet the expectations of society. We are bombarded with a feel-good culture that drills into us the message that negative people are draining and toxic. So now we have to deal with the emotions of guilt and betrayal by our own society. A society that is completely unprepared to deal with the emotions of a grieving person. What's more, we are repeatedly trying to justify our emotions to society, who wonder why we're not "better yet."

I was in a foggy funk for several days until I had an incredibly successful day in the gym with the support of my powerlifting team. I had accomplished the immense feat of deadlifting two-hundred-sixty-five pounds and surpassed my goal to lift my husband's body weight. After my team cheered me on and told me how they admired my inner and outer strength, I felt like I could do *anything*! I told Javier, "I felt you with me! Carpe Diem! Carpe Vita! *Let's go!*"

These stories are just some of the countless times I went from the mountain top to the dark valley, and vice versa. Processing the emotions felt during experiences like these in therapy was one of the many tools that helped me grieve healthily. Therapy helped me to see that it's okay to just be. It helped me to understand that as I navigate through this obstacle course of grief, some days I'm an agile sprinter, other days I'm making a slow crawl on my knees, and other days I may even take a giant leap backward. Even if I felt like my feet were trapped in tar, unable to move at all, I would reach into my tool kit and try my best to cope and coast through survival mode. Some days it was reaching out to my support system for a loved one to listen as I cry, other days it was running a 5K with my children in memory of their church friend and classmate, eight-year-old Kelsey.

Now, nine years a widow, all I know about the ebb and flow of grief is that it is a labyrinth from which each individual finds their own way and uses tools unique to them in the best way they know how. In the following chapters, I share the tools and coping mechanisms that helped my children and me as we treaded the waters of survival mode.

Chapter 14

What Do I Do With My Rage?

Disclosure: This letter may seem harsh and displays the rage of a widow. Keep in mind that I wrote this after two of my children were hospitalized with an incurable disease and they each spent a week in the ICU.

My dearest love, I'm sorry, but I can't help but feel rageful envy toward you. Sometimes I feel as though you had the better cards in this deal. I mean, you aren't hurting like I am. You don't have to hear our babies cry themselves to sleep missing you the way that I do, their pillows soaked in tears. Or go drag yourself from the couch only to tuck yourself into a bed of cold, empty loneliness. You didn't have to experience the trauma of watching your seven-year-old little daughter's fingers ferociously claw at your casket pleading, "I want to see Daddy! Why can't I see

81

Daddy?" She was unable to understand because she had seen both of her great-grandmothers and got to say good-bye to them at their funerals. You don't have to deal with the constant physical exhaustion of cleaning, cooking, maintaining a home, paying taxes, caring for chronically sick children, and on and on. I'm so done with single-parenting! I'm so done with the unceasing mental exhaustion of mourning and holding our mourning children as they search for you in your room, your closet, the workshop, or the yard. Their little faces are constantly searching for you out the window, asking, "Is Daddy cleaning the yard, Mommy? Is he coming home from work soon? Oh yeah, he's dead. Why can't I go to Heaven to see him, Mommy?"

I am in hell. I long for relief, even the faintest respite from this earthly torment that seems to have no end. I now understand his agony when Jesus cried out to His Father after nearly all had deserted him: "My God, my God, why have you forsaken me?" Javier, I am furiously envious of where you are and have often begged God to allow us to trade places, just for a little while, even though it makes no sense. I know I'm delirious with exhaustion, insomnia, and grief and not thinking clearly, but Javs, can you ask God if he will let you come back to me, even just temporarily to take over down here on earth, just for a little while? Because I'm done! I've put in my time, and it's only fair that God let us trade places so you can help me for a little while. Just a little while.

*A*nger? You better believe we feel anger. Anyone grieving knows, understands, and relates to these unavoidable stages of grief, especially anger. The rage I had at God was deafening. It was very healing for me to write about my raw grief. I could not make sense of how a loving God could give us the greatest, most blissful life as a family together and then allow it to all be ripped away from us. I felt rage for the life I now had to live—the life of a widow. I was now the mother of fatherless children who had no one to dance with at the father-daughter dance, no one to eat with at monthly "Dads and Donuts" school breakfasts, no father to throw the baseball with after school, and no baritone voice that whips their behavior into shape instantly. It was a life I couldn't help but resent. "It isn't fair" is something I know you have also yelled a thousand times. To experience such torment with no break or respite in sight makes many widows feel that God is not just cruel, but savagely wicked. In the midst of inescapable pain and anguish, it is completely normal and common for widows to lash out at God in anger or to even barter with God for the slightest of consolations for their desperate situation.

Our anger is only magnified by plaguing questions like: Why did a good father and husband have to die instead of a serial killer? Why did he have to die in such a calamitous, horrendous way? What did we ever do? Why do *my* children have to live without a father? Why do my children have to now bear the burden of being labeled an "at-risk youth" because they are now fatherless?

I was beyond angry at the journalist of the Houston Chronicle who wrote about the gruesome, gory details of my Javier's death during the last precious moments of his life . . . details which I dreadfully know my children will some-day read. I can go on and on about my anger, my pain, my despair. I can write whole books on the loneliness we widows feel despite being in a room full of family and friends.

During the most catastrophic event of their life, the widow is also desperately striving to cope with the unthink-able: identifying their spouse's body or trying to obtain med-ical or dental records to do so, receiving horrific details from the coroner's office, hearing that it must be a closed casket (thus denying them a final goodbye), and coping with trau-matic flashbacks of the final moments before their spouse's death. What's more, I've encountered several widows and widowers who lost a spouse *and* a child during an accident, widowers who lost their wife and unborn baby all at once, and widows who lost their husband and their own health from being in the same accident.

Perhaps the most difficult experience among my widowed friends in grief support groups was when someone discovered that their spouse had secrets, whether they were hiding an addiction, severe debt, adultery, or some other form of deceit. On top of the vast range of emotions from the death, they are now processing the rageful emotions that come from discov-ering their spouse's deception and betrayal.

There are also some widows consumed with rage because they are full of regret. They regret not getting their spouse adequate care for their illness. They regret the things they said during a huge fight on the day they died. They regret the betrayal or mistreatment they inflicted upon their spouse while they were living. They regret not encouraging their spouse to stay home and spend more time with their family rather than focusing so much on earning more money. They regret not saying "I love you" one last time. Or, like me, they regret not throwing their arms around their spouse and never letting them walk out that door to meet their death. And to add even more steaming fury on top of the heaping pile of rage, imagine feeling envious toward widows who don't regret what we regret. Or the added rage toward widows who had the "perfect" happy marriage, "perfect" family, or even "perfect" healthy children free of illness, behavior problems, or learning issues.

As widows wearily experience this wide range of emotions, they often feel as if their feet are encased in lead, with each step feeling progressively heavier than the last. We know all too well that processing emotions while grieving is physically, mentally, and emotionally exhausting, but no one prepares you for the endless yo-yo of emotions. The ups and downs of the mood swings. The tug-of-war between feeling the mountain-top highs one minute and then plummeting back down to the dark valley the next.

Some widows even feel angry at their spouses for dying. Despite how irrational that may sound, they blame their spouses because they have been left alone. Over the years, I have heard widows feel angry at their spouses for dying of heart attacks, sudden illnesses like COVID-19, cancers, elective surgeries, hypothermia, and even accidents.

I personally felt angry at my husband for dying when I needed him to help me with things that only he could do, and I also resented now having to learn how to do them myself. When he was alive, we excelled in what we were good at. Now suddenly, he was gone, and I had to learn how to do everything he used to do for us and more. I didn't want to be Mom *and* Dad—I didn't even know how! But I didn't have a choice, and knowing that hurt. I would look up to Heaven, asking him, "Javier, they're not obeying me, and I need you to tell these boys to listen to me! Where am I supposed to take the car to get it fixed when the dealership keeps overcharging me? I need you to fix the water heater that's leaking! Who do I trust to fix these things without you telling me that I can? How am I supposed to talk to your sons about puberty and 'man stuff?' I need you!" On some of my darkest days, I prayed my way through my rage because that was all I knew how to do.

Throughout this book, you will hear me steer the widow toward two things: processing emotions in therapy and the use of healthy coping strategies as a means of therapeutic healing. One sad truth I have come to realize is that grief education is sorely lacking in our society, and it benefits all people to learn about grief. There is not only a stigma against seeking mental health treatment, such as therapy, but there is also a cultural and societal pressure to not feel our negative emotions. There is an immense pressure forced upon the grieving widow, whether implicit or explicit, to "feel better" or "move on." When those who are grieving suppress their emotions for society's comfort, they are vastly disrupting and inhibiting their natural grief response, which multiplies their suffering. These social constraints that are imposed by culture and society on those who are grieving force the griever to feel alienated, marginalized, and ever more sorrowful. What's more, it causes those who are grieving to doubt their own hearts and wonder, why don't I feel better yet, the way society expects me to?

What does society need to offer those who are grieving? When I asked myself this question, the first thing that came to mind was the fact that there is so little known about the trauma of grief unless one has endured it. To help those who mourn, society must be prepared to provide us with a nurturing place to rest our hearts from the battlefield of our minds. In short, in this age of positivity, our society must not be so quick to influence our emotions toward "feeling better," and instead create a safe place to allow the widow to simply *be*.

Grief is not linear. It is a tangled, muddled mess of stages that interchange and interweave continuously throughout the days, weeks, months, and years ahead. It is healthy to experience each stage of grief fully. These stages are not to be avoided, skipped over, or misunderstood. It is okay to not be okay. It is okay to feel extreme, raw emotions such as rage, sadness, depression, and despair. A pastor once tried to prevent me from feeling anger by telling me that he was not angry at God for his dad's death because all people die and Heaven is the ultimate goal. It's as if he wanted me to avoid feeling any of my natural emotions and instantly skip right to acceptance. Firstly, there is no comparison whatsoever between his grief in losing his father and my grief in losing my husband at twenty-nine years old with three children under seven. It is nonsensical to compare one person's grief to another.

Secondly, it is important to recognize and communicate when someone is being counterproductive to your healing by trying to force you to suppress your emotions. This may be done through judgment, coercion, or scrutiny toward you. We will discuss later how vital it is to find counselors and friends who are best at helping, not hindering, your grief. We've all heard the phrase, "Those who grieve well, live well." You have been through enough, and you deserve to grieve well.

I was asked recently how widows cope with anger and pain. I responded, "We feel it, let it go, and repeat. Over and over and over again." The pain and anger will be felt and released a thousand times, and each time it will feel a little lighter. The hope I wish to share with you is that you will not feel like this forever. I know it doesn't feel like it today, in the wake of the storm, but the pain is temporary. It comes and it goes.

Chapter 15
Seeking Professional Help in Therapy & Counseling

My dearest love, today is Valentine's Day. Once, when your best friend heard how you had flowers, chocolates, and a bear delivered to your wife and daughter every year for Valentine's Day, he teased you saying, "Javi, tone it down, bro, you're starting to make us husbands look bad!" When Daniella and I received our Valentine's Day gifts just a few days after your death, I nearly collapsed to my knees as family and friends caught me from crumbling to the ground.

How will I carry on after the loss of my soulmate whose love made me feel so important, so beautiful, so strong, so valuable? I miss you for more than just having someone by my side as I excelled in the things I was once good at. I also miss you for the things that I am unable to do that you did so well, like the practical things you looked forward to teaching our sons: your leadership and discipline; or how quickly you could change a tire, fix the water heater, or renovate the kitchen; your hobby of woodworking, making picnic tables and shelves from scratch for the kids' rooms; making the perfect brisket, (I recall your dedication in smoking it to perfection all night long for your sister Angelica's wedding). You are also missed for the way you loved to cook dinner for your siblings growing up, exactly the way your son Tony now does! And the giddiness in your face when you and your brother Mario performed the most outstanding fireworks display for your family on your parents' land. But it goes beyond all those minutiae. It's also during each moment throughout this journey of life without you. This absence of you is felt so deeply that it penetrates my soul, deep within my bones, in the very fiber of my being, and in the deep, unnamable beyond that lies within us all.

Who do I run to when our son scores a goal? Who do I run to tell when our child who struggles with dyslexia reads his first novel (The Hobbit, your favorite)? Who do I run to hug when I just finished singing for an audience in your memory? I know it's cliché, but losing my soulmate truly feels like I've lost my soul and heart . . . for what is a soul and heart to a human being? It is your passion, your drive, your grit! To lose this spark, especially one as luminous as

yours, Javs, leaves life so drab. How can I handle Christ-
mas, anniversaries, and our kid's graduations without you?
I am numb and can't see anything past the pain. Carry me,
my love, I'm literally too weak to stand. I need help.

The full impact of sudden loss is never realized right away. Trauma is so shocking to the mind (and body) that it tries to protect itself from lethal levels of pain with a sort of numbing amnesia. It is as if the widow is in an altered reality as their brain processes the trauma. However, once the veil is lifted and the pain of our trauma is felt, we need help working through our grief. There is no shame in getting prescription medication to treat insomnia, depression, attention deficit disorder, and "widow brain."

If you google "widow brain," you will find that it is a state of mental fog following the death of a spouse. The widow's brain has become so overwhelmed from managing the effects of the cataclysmic trauma that it struggles to carry out routine duties. Much like a computer's CPU that glitches after non-stop churning, the brain in survival mode "turns off" certain switches to preserve energy. Additionally, despite taking medications for insomnia, you may find that poor quality of sleep drastically affects our cognitive abilities. In my experience, any sleep is better than no sleep at all. Even the slightest amount of sleep deprivation, interrupted sleep, or medication-induced sleep affects our physical and mental health.

Over the years, I have come across some widows and widowers who are opposed to therapy. This saddens me. I didn't like the first therapist I went to either. Just think: what if you never went to another doctor again, all because *one* doctor gave bad medical care? We would never say, "I don't care if my femur is broken in five places, I'll never go to another doctor again!" The same applies with doctors of the mind. Just as we work with an orthopedist for physical training to repair our fractured femur, we must work with a doctor of the mind to help us repair our fractured mind. If it feels uncomfortable or we don't like their bedside manner, simply choose another one until you find the best fit for you.

Please, if you get nothing else from this book, my prayer is that you glean this: One of the greatest ways we can love ourselves and our children is by providing a healthy and stable environment. Now that we are both the primary caretakers *and* the head of the household, we must be vigilant in maintaining the emotional and mental well-being of our home. By actively working on healing our own minds and our children's minds with a counselor, we are also demonstrating to our children the importance of maintaining our health mentally and emotionally—a valuable tool that will help them into adulthood. We are also showing our children the importance of caring for all of the lives under their roof, which will affect our grandchildren down the line. By working through the process of our own mental healing, we are providing our babies with the greatest gift: the best self that we can possibly be. Another type of widow I have experienced is the perfect widow. I have encountered countless widows (myself included) who felt they should never waver from playing the part of the saint by portraying anger, weakness, frustration, or doubt. This particular type of widow believes if they falter in the slightest from steadfast fidelity, they are sinning by questioning God's plan. However, after time passes, the light begins to dim from the leaden pressure to appear heroic to all around them. Counselors don't say, "Allow yourself to go through all of the stages of grief except if your religion says otherwise." No, they tell us to freely feel our emotions as we undergo all of the stages of grief throughout the process.

For many widows, reading this next paragraph may feel foreign to you because you are not at this place yet. You may think: I can't imagine enjoying myself again, because if I smile or laugh, that means I'm forgetting them. I used to think the same. The very first time I laughed after he died, I ran to my room and cried for hours because I felt so guilty for forgetting him. I now realize that I could never forget him, not even for a moment, but it took *many* therapy sessions to work through my survivor's guilt.

Oftentimes we survivors feel that we don't deserve to have fun since we are still living life and our spouse is dead. For those who struggle with taking even the tiniest steps toward grief work, you can start with rewarding yourself even for the smallest, incremental steps toward it. As I said, grief work is by far the hardest work you will ever do. After finding the right counselor, reward yourself, because you are loving and caring for yourself—something that does not come easily to widows. Whether you affirm yourself in words or treat yourself to something or go somewhere, it's all part of the process.

Personally speaking, it took me a *very* long time to do this. In fact, I still struggle with it today. It's hard to tell myself nice things, almost as if I think I don't deserve to hear it. I still struggle to get out the words: Julie, I am proud of you. One thing I did to reward myself recently was buy myself a coffee when I took my daughter out. Usually, I don't buy myself anything because I don't want to spend money on myself. Instead, the gift for me is the time shared with my kids. But this time I did it! When I walked up, holding two drinks, my daughter said, "Yay! You deserve it, Mommy! I'm proud of you!" Tears welled up in our eyes as we went on to chat in a British accent about the joys of life. I had no idea that being kind to myself would also be a gift to my children to see their mother happy. It was a beautiful moment in my life when my daughter taught me to love myself. Lo and behold, the next day, after nearly nine years of avoiding writing the first chapter of this book, I finally decided to sit down and write it. I'm so proud of myself.

It was a long process to allow myself to have fun. The second summer after Javier died, his parents invited me and the kids on a trip to San Francisco. Allowing myself to go was the first time I allowed myself to have fun. We visited Javier's family, who welcomed us with open arms. What an adventure! We made tie-dye shirts, saw the San Francisco bridge, felt the frigid Pacific Ocean and the sand beneath our toes, explored the famous San Francisco Aquarium, and much more. I had no idea how much we needed it, but somehow Javier's parents did.

So please, allow yourself to be proud of yourself. I am proud of you, even if you are not proud of you. It certainly would've helped me to hear that years ago from a fellow widow.

Lastly, as we course through this grieving process with all of its ups and downs, let us keep in mind that past traumas affect how we process present grief. If we have experienced trauma in our past, whether it be childhood trauma, war/combat trauma, relationship trauma, or other trauma, we often revert back to old habits and patterns that we used to cope. Furthermore, if we have a history of not processing our grief in the past, why would we start now? The patterns we set for healing from trauma teach our loved ones by example how to grieve well, and it can start today, whether we're fifty-five or twenty-five.

Even as a young bride, I saw the advantages of healing in therapy. In my early twenties, I had the bad habit of acting like our problems didn't exist by avoiding them when life became overwhelming. It took hard work in therapy to learn that, not only was I hurting the people who loved me, but I needed new coping strategies and ways of communicating how I felt rather than shutting the truth out. Actively working in therapy to heal is one of the greatest intergenerational gifts we can give to our children, grandchildren, and great-grandchildren. What a gift for our great-grandchildren to one day say to their children, "Your great-grandma (or great-grandpa) was a young widow with children and was one of the strongest, most inspiring people I've ever known! And you're related!"

Chapter 16

Self-Sabotage &
Avoiding Toxicity

My dearest love, why did it have to be you? You promised me, "Julie, we'll sit rocking on our porch and watch our great-grandchildren run around the yard, completely unphased by how gravity has wreaked havoc upon our bodies, and thank God for all the life we've shared together." You were the selfless one. You were my brave, chivalrous protector! You were the chef! How can I possibly mimic your perfect ravioli or slow-roasted Texas brisket? How can I possibly replace the many things you would have taught our children throughout your lifetime? I told you so many times that it should have been me, but each time I would hear you say, "No, Julie, don't say that my love."

My only consolation was when your sweet mother told me how much you loved me and lived for your family after I said, "I wish Javier had never followed me to Houston, then he would still be alive!" Your strong, beautiful, saintly mother replied, "No, Julie, never say that. God brought you together. You were his world. You and the children were his everything." Her words unraveled the burden that felt like a ship's anchor from around my neck. Her words allowed me to breathe for the first time in years. I felt her forgiveness release me from the vice of painful self-loathing. I felt her love heal me. My love, it felt as though you were saying to me to let it go. I now see so clearly why you loved so deeply while you were alive—your parents taught you how. It is impossible to put this miraculous healing into words, but I know you felt it too.

There's so much to be said about widows who, simply put, stop loving themselves. Maybe they have survivor's guilt and feel they don't deserve to be the spouse who's left behind. Maybe they feel their spouse would do a much better job raising their children, maintaining the home, paying the taxes, haggling with the repairman, and preparing holiday family gatherings with all the shopping, cooking, and gift wrapping. Maybe they feel their spouse would better mask their feelings around others, especially their kids.

More often than not, widows are so busy caring for their children (and sometimes elderly parents) that they feel their own life is not worth any bit of extra care. When a widow is forced to sit with these feelings of self-loathing day in and day out, it can become a breeding ground where toxic, racing thoughts run rampant. This is a long chapter because, not only do widows torture themselves, but they often lack the awareness and confidence needed to start the steps toward loving and caring for themselves.

What's more, it's difficult to avoid what's obviously harmful to us when we are in a state of utter despair. I remember calling my dad while curled up in the corner of my closet, clenching the wedding ring that firemen found in the rubble, as I whimpered through the phone, "Dad, I can't smell Javier's scent on his clothes anymore! I can't see anything through all the pain!" The grief masks every glimmer of hope that other people see, and other people can't seem to understand why you *can't* see it!

For many widows, we hate our changed lives so much that we lose all awareness to care for ourselves, and self-sabotage or self-destruction settles in. Sometimes it is because we are in so much pain that we do not feel worthy of love. Sometimes it is because we feel envy that our spouse gets to rest as we toil endlessly with relentless suffering and unwavering responsibility. Sometimes it's because we feel guilty that our spouse died young and we feel undeserving of the gift of life (and may feel like we're squandering this gift). Sometimes, we hate what our lives have become when we are around our friends' families, who remind us of the bliss that our lives used to be. If you recognize and relate to any of the aforementioned, find peace in the fact that self-realization or self-awareness is the first step to beginning to change our behaviors.

It is no secret to those who are mourning how prevalent it is for widows to "self-medicate" with behaviors such as drug use, alcohol use, sex, or any other self-destructive behavior to temporarily ease the pain of grief. If the behaviors or activities are not inherently destructive, they can become destructive if not monitored and maintained. Even if widows previously had the knowledge to be mindful of moderation, it is particularly difficult to uphold in the midst of their deep pain and grief. Education on this subject from a counselor is what is crucial. Widows are always careful not to cross the line with other widows who are grieving. There is a fine line between encouraging other widows to grieve however they feel they need to and discouraging them from harming themselves. Even when we fellow widows understand the reason *why* other widows feel the need for these self-destructive behaviors, we still struggle with intervening because we do not want to hurt the widow more during this delicate time. It has always been heartbreakingly difficult for me to stand by powerless as others destroy themselves. Although I try my best to lovingly steer them toward seeking mental-health professionals and healthy coping strategies, ultimately, I know they need to find their own paths to follow.

While I personally navigated through the ups and downs of the stages of grief, I wish I could say that I always grieved healthily; that I always surrounded myself with family, friends, community, and coworkers who loved me, wanted the best for me, and saw the best in me, but I didn't. One of my best friends Liz told me that I once sent my friends a group text message telling them all that I could no longer be around them because it was just too painful. I had zero memory of this and had completely forgotten doing it. I apparently felt forgotten by my friends and decided to lash out at all of them. This not only hurt my friends but hurt me. I later discovered that self-isolation was one of the ways I was self-sabotaging. When I cut myself off from the people that loved me, I slipped further from my safety net into the raging waters. However, this newfound self-awareness was a pivotal moment where I began changing my behavior from punishing myself with isolation to communicating with my friends about the depth of my pain and loneliness. I chose to let love in. I had to learn to identify within myself when I needed to talk to adults who love me, when I needed a hug, and when I needed to cry.

I also learned that communicating my needs to a loved one was one of the best ways to avoid toxicity. I did this by surrounding myself and my children with people who allowed me to share my emotions openly and inspired an emotionally stable environment. For some, this may mean making *all new* friends. For others, this may even mean temporarily placing distance between specific friends or family during this delicate time. If you set healthy boundaries for your family and friends and they are still overstepping those boundaries, it is time to discern whether you should be surrounding yourself with them while you are in such an emotionally compromised state.

Widows are in such a vulnerable state of mind that it can be difficult to be assertive and speak up for what's best for the well-being of themselves and their children. But *be assertive.* No one knows what you need but you. Although the people closest to you cannot possibly imagine your pain, in their minds, they believe their advice is helping ease it. Sometimes, their advice can be harsh and critical but is exactly what you need to hear. Other times, you may want to be left alone and aren't ready to hear it because you are angry, exhausted, in pain. If someone is telling you that you shouldn't be sleeping all day or eating an entire carton of ice cream, it's okay to be assertive and tell them you're not in a place to hear criticism because you're just in survival mode. You're just putting one foot in front of the other right now.

Even if you know they're right and you shouldn't binge eat your pain away, it feels insensitive and hurts when someone judges your behaviors while your life is upside down. Even if they have experienced profound loss and do understand on some level, each individual processes pain differently. Even if their spouse died in exactly the same way, they have the same number of children, and the same amount of family support, it is still impossible to compare mourning. Above all, telling a person to stop a specific unhealthy behavior isn't going to magically stop them in their tracks and force them to stop. They not only have to *want* to stop, they have to have the willpower to stop.

Another issue widows experience, worse than bad advice, is people's rude attitude. They don't just say, "You shouldn't eat an entire carton of ice cream," they say it with a rude tone of voice. I've always visualized people's rude attitude to be a toxin that subtly permeates the whole environment, potentially causing your peaceful mental space to quickly be overcome. If you do not want to develop an aversion to this person who is important to you, you must find the strength to communicate gracefully what's specifically harmful to your grieving process. The antidote to their toxic attitude is a mixture of communication and love. This means communicating lovingly what you need for your mental and spiritual well-being by saying something like, "I know you love me, but I can't hear things like that right now. It isn't helping." If what they want to do is help, telling them that they are not helping will give them clarity in seeing your boundary. For example, one of my family members knocked on the door one day and said in a harsh tone, "You can't cry all day, every day. There's still life to live. You're twenty-nine years old!" I asked them to please ask me first before doing or saying things to my children while we were grieving. So that they did not become defensive, I also reassured them that it wasn't any sort of personal attack, but that I was simply speaking up for what I needed at that time.

Family and friends who are closest to us are the hardest to communicate things like this to because we often revert back to our roles in the relationship. In addition, oftentimes they are grieving and hurting too because they either were close to your beloved or they feel powerless to your pain. Rather than bottling it up inside and blowing up at them later, it's best to communicate. Believe it or not, speaking up for ourselves is a form of self-love that takes practice. We have to find the inner strength to repeatedly practice speaking up for ourselves and our children. If others still aren't respecting your boundaries, you may need to reassess if they deserve to gain access to you, which is especially difficult if you are dependent upon their help or care.

Finally, communicating to loved ones exactly what you need is vital. Understandably, widows are so dazed by the fog of grief that they don't even know what it is they need, much less how to articulate it. An example of this for me was when my family and friends would say things like, "Julie, are you sleeping and eating enough?" I responded by asking if they could take the kids to the park so that I can take a nap, instead of saying what I wanted to say: "My husband just died! *Of course not*!" Enveloping yourself and your children in an emotionally stable environment with people who love and support healthy grieving is like your safety net during survival mode.

SECTION 4:
Self-Care Spiritually

Chapter 17

Your Safety Net & Support System

My dearest love, how can I put pen to paper to describe the precious moments in which you breathed your last breath and life left your body . . . our body. After you kissed me goodbye the morning you left for work, I woke up later to prepare the children's breakfast and lay out their cute outfits for their friend's birthday party later that day.

Suddenly, I received a call. Your mother told me that the plant where you worked had an explosion. I will never forget the way she told me, "Julie, you have to go to him!" Waiting for her to arrive to watch our babies and making the short drive over to your plant felt like an eternity. I cried out to God and to you during the entire drive, beg-

ging God to hold me up. I cried out from my soul, "I'm coming, my love, hang on!" The memory of the police cars, fire trucks, and ambulance barricades shielding the public from the massive blaze and plumes of smoke will forever be embedded in my memory.

When I arrived, I begged the officer on the scene to let me pass, but he funneled me and other employees from the plant to the hotel across the street. Each passing hour that I waited to hear that they'd found you was like a knife being twisted in my chest. From the early morning hours until the sun went down, I waited. As I prayed throughout the day, I just knew that the first responders would walk in with the joyful news that they had found you safely tucked away in some closet, like some of the survivors on September 11, who were found barricaded under debris. And then . . . the indescribable moment that my heart stopped: the chief of the fire department walked in. My family and Father Pilsner huddled around me as my safety net as the chief revealed that they had found the remains of my husband, and a close friend of his had been flown to the hospital with burns on over 75 percent of his body.

The moments that followed are a foggy blur as if I am recalling the events of a dream. When those words left his mouth, my heart stopped and my body went limp. I didn't feel alive anymore; I felt his words had killed me. Suddenly, my sister Natalie and I collapsed on the floor in shock. My very first thoughts were: Oh God, our children! What do I do? How will I live?

A healthy support system is your safety net. These are the people closest to you that you can cry with and vent to, and that you can depend on for the hard stuff like childcare, cooking, and cleaning. These people are the special human beings who will hold you up after you bury your soulmate.

For me, these were the people who were with me as I stood outside the inferno of the chemical plant and waited all day in hopes that the firemen would tell me they found him safely pinned under some rubble. These were the people who held me up during the news interview. These were the people who carried me out of the building when I received the news from the chief of the fire department that my husband's dead body had been found. Not just my parents and siblings, but also my dear friends Cynthia and Larry Sepulveda, whose sixteen-year-old son (and my student), Jose, had died from sudden illness just a few years before. These are the people who see a need and lovingly act. I didn't have to ask my mom to make me soup, she just did it, the same way she did after my children's births. I didn't have to ask my dad to drive miles across Houston to sleep on my floor (he insisted it was better for his back), help with the kids, and attend every important meeting to get my affairs in order. The luxury for your children to have involved grandparents is seriously underrated.

It is also important that your safety net includes people who will share happy stories with your children of the person their father or mother once was. I loved how my mom sat and painted with her grandkids and told stories of how wonderful a father he was, and how he loved to cook amazing barbequed brisket, chicken, corn on the cob, homemade tortillas, and fresh apple pie! I love sitting around his family's table, sharing a meal and love on a Sunday afternoon—as his sister, brother, and parents share stories with our children of the man he was. Seeing their Aunt Angelica's face light up as she describes how their father was an incredible friend in high school and college to everyone who knew him. Or, how much she liked to tease her brother by buying the noisiest musical toys when they were little babies, just to annoy her big brother. Laughing at the fact that each time the kids clanged on their drums and flutes he would jokingly cry out, "ANGI!" And, telling them how he was a kid at heart who didn't want to throw away his favorite childhood Ninja-Turtle blanket (faded beyond recognition) even well past college! And there were also all the stories from their grandfather. Just the other day, after a day at the science museum, we went to lunch with my dad. I sat with a mouthful of sandwich and just listened to my dad share stories with his grandchildren about the incredible man their father was. His grandchildren looked at him intently as he told them all about how their father was a brilliant chemist who gave presentations in the very same science museum we were just at! To hear the joy in my dad's voice as he described how their dad entertained an audience full of kids with shining eyes that lit up as their dad dipped a rose into liquid nitrogen and shattered it like glass was a true treasure! It was a gift worth more than mountains made of gold to hear my own father speak with such high esteem and respect for the man their father was. In fact, the way my dad told the story to his grandchildren made them feel as though their grandfather's hero was *their own father*!

This is the type of safety net one needs. It doesn't have to be many people. Maybe it's just one person. I also want to recognize and acknowledge that hearing all of this may be painful to some of you because you so desperately need a safety net of loving people, but you don't at this time. If this is the case for you, sometimes finding a community that can nurture you is what's needed. Whether it's a therapist, pastor, religious community, grief community, community of like-minded people, or new friends, seeking out those who can love us is vital to healthy grieving.

Chapter 18

Creativity— the Art of the Spirit

You may be thinking: Creativity? My highest form of creativity was when my soulmate and I co-created our children out of love, but now that they're gone, I lack all motivation or desire to create anything. For some time after his death, I struggled to see other pregnant mothers or newborn babies because we had lost our unborn baby months before my husband died. Overjoyed with the new life we created, we held one another in the doctor's office as we witnessed his little heartbeat on the ultrasound monitor. Javier said to me, "He looks like a John Paul to me."

After John Paul and Javier died, my art portrayed emptiness, with paintings of empty arms and abstract voids of nothingness. One of the most profound discoveries in my *grief journey* was realizing that my creativity has been a powerful, cathartic resource that has been vital to my grieving process.

Creativity is spiritual therapy, a form of prayer in an offering of ourselves, a spiritual medicine of the soul. Whether I am using my gifts to sing, write, or speak publicly, I am prayerfully revealing a piece of my soul uniquely created by God that can never be replicated. You may choose to express yourself through painting, drawing, pottery, sewing, music, crafts, stand-up, acting, or other activities.

It is also sad how underrated this is to the grieving process. Like play therapy, I call creativity the "play of the spirit," where our spirit can express its unique self through play. God is creative. And since human beings are made in the image of God, our creativity is always spiritual. When we are expressing our own unique creativity, our soul speaks and reveals the beautiful inner-workings of our spirit. In other words, when we are creating, we are revealing our true, authentic selves as God intended us to be. After all, I can't help but wonder what God is revealing in his own unique, artistic expression when I look at the diverse creatures of the world; creatures like a platypus compared to a swan, a naked mole-rat compared to a bunny, an aye-aye compared to a puppy, or a blob-fish compared to a vibrant betta fish. Creativity is an *opus spiritus*, meaning it is a work of the spirit. Over the years, I noticed that when I neglected the creative part of myself, I felt as though something was missing.

One unique way my parents fostered this creativity within my siblings and I was when my dad and step-mom brought us to a group called Creativity led by Mary Whipple, a licensed therapist. Here we gathered together, sharing our creative works, including art, poetry, singing, acting, and storytelling. It was here that I discovered the power of spirituality flowing from creativity.

God puts beautiful souls on our path to help us express our creativity. My baby sister, Michelle, inspired me with her incredible artistry, from pottery to oil on canvas to crocheting amazing creations. She inspired me to start making music again. A couple of years ago, after struggling with artist's block for some time, I met Donna, a stained-glass master artist who inspired me by sharing her art all while balancing life as a Navy veteran, mother, and wife. Now my daughter, Daniella, is a stained-glass artist too! As Donna shared her work, she shared pieces of her soul, which lit a spark that spread like wildfire on our street! Donna had rekindled the gift of creativity within us all.

We got together one hot summer day in July, sat on giant painter's quilts on her lawn, and painted together as neighbors, adults and children alike. After that day, my kid's Aunt Natalie and Uncle Orlando taught them how to forge wooden swords in his woodworking shop (one of their dad's favorite hobbies). The kids also got to do seasonal arts and crafts with their cousins. More recently, my teenage children's dynamic art teacher, an Army combat veteran turned master artist, has been the catalyst that set my children's love for art in motion. Now I'm swimming in artwork scattered all around the house!

Lastly, I want to reassure those who feel hopeless in rekindling their creativity that they're not alone. I remember clearly how broken my spirit felt at the thought of creating again until I read a line in a poem written by Saint Mother Teresa of Calcutta entitled "Do It Anyway":

"What you spend years creating, others could destroy overnight. Create anyway."

How could she say it so casually? I spent a decade building a beautiful life, a future with my soulmate with whom I planned to spend a lifetime. We created our children, built up our marriage, our careers, our household, our faith with love, and I'm expected to "create anyway" after witnessing its destruction vaporize in a nanosecond? It took surrendering my will to ask God to help me want to try again. I have no doubt that discovering my new unique creativity has saved my life after my husband's death. As the analogy goes, we are all a little instrument in the hand of God, and he is composing the symphony. All of the joyful and sorrowful experiences of my life have inspired me to create and share my creativity. For all you know, you may be doing the same for someone else.

Chapter 19

The Nourishment
of Mother Nature

*My dearest love, I remember seven days before your death when we were on retreat and it was my turn to zip-line above the pine trees of the spruce forest when you yelled up to me from our crowd of friends below, "Julie, don't be afraid! Just do it! **Let go and let God!**" Though I couldn't see you, I could hear you; the confidence in your voice showing you believed in me! Your words were all I needed to remind me that God has me. I let go! As I sailed above the trees, feeling the wind blow through my hair and the sun on my face, I soaked God into my soul, thanking him for all that I have and for all that is.*

I have often thought back to that distinct memory and the fear and exhilaration I felt. All these years later, and those words you yelled up to me, are still the driving force to not be afraid and trust God. Each time I have returned to nature and felt the sun on my face, the wind through my hair, and the smell and sounds of creation, I feel your presence too.

For me, the most beautiful memory of all was when we went on a little stroll and saw two oak trees that had grown so close together that their tree trunks had merged into one and you said to me, "Look Julz, the closer they got to God, the closer they got to each other—until they were one." The memory of your words and the way that you looked at me when you said them will stay alive in my spirit forever. Thank you for reminding me of God's healing love found in nature.

I recently read an article about how some Canadian psychiatrists are prescribing National Park passes because they know that being connected to nature can be as good as taking antidepressants. One of the easiest ways to reset our minds and calm our spirits is to be in nature. The truth is, we are creatures meant to be among creation, not boxed up in four walls all day like a rat in a cage. Whether it's by feeling the sun on our faces, the grass under our toes, or the soil between our fingers, human beings are physiologically altered when they step into nature.

Perhaps it is children who are the better teachers of this, and we parents are their students. When my children were young, they would encourage me to splash in the puddles, help earthworms cross the road, and jump fearlessly into the freezing river. We have since enjoyed mother nature in a variety of ways from playing in the snow, ice skating, skiing, swimming, kayaking, tobogganing, and even ice fishing. I have learned that it doesn't have to be an amazing mountain climb; it can be a simple jog with our dog to our local duck pond, swimming at Galveston beach, or kayaking with friends at Stillhouse Lake.

It can be challenging to convince all the kids at once to go out in nature, so I would often prepare a delicious smorgasbord picnic with their favorite foods to convince them. Afterward, my happier, lighter children would look up to me and say, "Thank you, Mommy, I needed that!" As a parent, I innately felt that we as human beings need fresh air, vitamin D from the sun's rays, and the mental/spiritual nourishment that only Mother Nature provides.

Chapter 20

Spirituality & Prayer

The following is my own personal grief experience.

    I will never forget the very first time I questioned God's love for me. Soon after I buried my husband, I was sitting alone on the couch, when suddenly I had a flashback to my first college missionary trip in a small, rural town near Durango, Mexico. I fell seriously ill, most likely due to water sanitation issues, and would have died without intervention. The director, and leader of Youth Ambassadors of Christ, Brian Johnson, received word that I was so ill from dehydration and fever that I was hallucinating and talking to a man in the wall. Brian then took me on a rescue mission, from a random man's pickup truck to a bus to a humble makeshift hospital in Durango. On the bus ride packed with people, I began to dry heave, and my heart began to race and flutter because my stomach had nothing left to purge (even the bile in my stomach had turned to foam). I slumped in my seat, barely conscious, and said to God in my heart, "Please, if you help me survive this, I will do your work."

I snapped out of my flashback and back to my reality as a young widow, and I cried out again to God, "Is this what you saved me for? A life full of suffering?" I suddenly understood and related to the words of St. Theresa of Avila who suffered from epileptic temporal lobe seizures for many years: "If this is how You treat your friends, it is no wonder You have so few!" I understood like never before Jesus' plea to his Father, "My God, my God, why hast thou forsaken me?" (Matthew 27:46). Like a victim of a gunshot wound whose shock begins to fade, I slid into the fetal position, my entire body cramped in pain, as I cried out, "*Why, God? Why?* Take this suffering from me!"

No one was prepared to tell me, a young widow, that it is *okay* to feel rage one moment and hope the next; that feeling it *all* (whenever I need to feel it) is okay; that it is completely understandable that there were many nights I did not want to unclench my fists and relinquish my fury, hate, and despair. I now see that freely feeling my broad range of emotions was all part of the cyclical process of grieving. Yes, it is true that when I feel rage and despair, I am visiting the dark void, but I *have* to visit this place. I have to sit with my anger. I have to feel my pain and suffering before I can let it go and undergo some level of healing. If I suppress my feelings, I only make myself sicker and magnify my pain and suffering.

I discovered years later that the key for me, personally, was remembering that it is only a *visit* to the void and not a permanent dwelling place. Although I returned to this chasm of gloom again and again, with each wave of life pressing me under, I learned that I cannot stay there indefinitely. Oftentimes, this was easier said than done because the abyss was a place where I felt stuck in cement. As I said previously, I set up many "makeshift tents" in my visits to the abyss, and as I sat there I would feel it, let it go, and repeat. The self-discovery to not stay indefinitely in the abyss was due to my overwhelming desire to be available to my children. I came to the realization that when I was zoned-out in the abyss of pain, bitterness, and resentment, I disappeared.

I ultimately discovered that what they needed from me was me.

On top of all the loss that the widow is enduring, many also struggle with grieving the loss of their faith and religion, whether temporarily or permanently. Soon after his death, I found it hard to pray. Most of my prayers before his death made perfect sense and came naturally to me. Talking to God used to be like second nature to me, as if I were speaking to my dad or mom. However, after his death, I felt like I was speaking to a stranger. The trust in our relationship had been shattered because I felt betrayed and unloved. I struggled to thank God. Most of my prayers had become frantic pleas and the ramblings of a lunatic who desperately needed help with raising three little children, maintaining a house, and carrying out all the domestic duties, all while working as a high school teacher.

I know what you're thinking: If I don't have time for mental health counselors, how will I find time to pray? The truth and reality is, God doesn't need our prayers. God doesn't need anything. Our prayers, our speaking to God, is for us, not God. If God (or whatever name you call the Creator) is the source of love and of all that is good, then when we cut ourselves off from that source of love, we are hurting ourselves. God wants us to have true happiness and true peace that the world cannot give, but when we cut off this connection and stop replenishing our hearts with God, we begin to feel more lost and alone than ever. It is as if we are so miserable that we are willingly punishing ourselves by forcing ourselves to stay in a dark place, separated from God. Every widow understands that we do it because the pain washes us under, but this is the dichotomy: surrender to the pain. The only way out of it is to go through it.

When I visualized my own unique spirituality, I visualized little Julie holding the hand of God throughout my life . . . until I struggled with the grief of losing my husband. It didn't happen right away. It was more of a slow change, where over time I subtly loosened my grip on God's hand and pulled ever so slowly away from him. If you grew up in the Church the way I did, you may have heard things like, "If you turn your back on God's light, you shrink. And if you turn toward God's light, you grow." When we turn our backs on God, we are hurting ourselves. Although I had heard phrases like this since kindergarten Bible school, nothing could prepare me for the raw truth these little phrases possessed more than the experience of widowhood. Although I never turned completely away from God, I still inadvertently cut myself off from God's grace when I stopped speaking to him. When I stopped filling my heart and soul with all that is purely good, the way I had unceasingly for twenty-nine years, I went from beginning each prayer with, "Daddy I love you. Thank you for . . .," to instead saying, "You obviously don't care about me, God, because if you did, you would not have treated me, our babies, and most of all, my Javier this way."

For what felt like a year, I struggled with my faith. Hitting rock-bottom is to feel completely and utterly lost. And that is exactly where I found myself: rock-bottom. I was a dandelion seed blowing in the wind, completely unsure of who I was without God or where I was going to land and take root. I landed on rocky soil many times throughout that year without a rain cloud in sight.

One particular day, I couldn't recognize who I had become, and I couldn't take the pain of my life any longer, so I cried out to God from the depths of the abyss. I asked God to give me strength to leave this desolate mindset I had found myself stuck in. Just like that, God delivered me and renewed my heart and soul within his soul, and I had a direct lifeline to love and all that is good once again. I was restored to the real Julie and felt awakened in the Spirit of God. After I attended confession at UST, the priest lovingly told me, "Welcome home. God loves you." How could he know I felt lost when I mentioned nothing of it? I felt it was God telling me this, and have never let go of his hand since.

People who have experienced hell on earth, who have suffered in the rawest, most obscene experiences of cold, arid misery, and anguish, yet find their way back to God, are some of the most profound people of faith I have ever met. They clasp God's hand tighter than anyone because they know the misery of what it's like to be without God. That is how I view my faith now. That doesn't mean I don't get frustrated with God from time to time, like when two of my children were diagnosed six weeks apart with a lifelong, incurable disease and both had to be hospitalized for a week. God can take my moods because he knows we're close like that. A pastor even told me once that it doesn't matter what we scream at God, he can take it. My Dad told me a story like this recently. He said, "When you were a little toddler and would throw tantrums on the ground, it didn't upset me or make me love you any less." God is always ready with open arms to receive us, no matter how much bitter anger and resentment we carry.

Chapter 21

The Gift of Giving

My Dearest Love, seven days before you died and left this world forever, you and I served at a retreat for teenagers to help them deepen their faith in God. You gave a profound speech, telling the young audience, "If I die tomorrow, just know one thing: God loves you! That will never, ever change." The phrase on your shirt read, "Face to Face," with the Scripture verse referencing meeting God face to face at the end of life. You were wearing this shirt the day you died. Even more profound, I was coincidentally wearing this shirt the day you died too.

My Love, how could I ever possibly be me again? Not when the "other half" of me has died. We were one flesh, remember? One being. Now, there is only a hollowed-out-half of me walking around, barely alive—like a survivor of a shipwreck trying to keep my head above water with each passing wave of life, trying to grieve, trying to cope, trying to survive. And, though it's unfathomably discouraging to have continuous, unyielding waves pushing me back undersea, I find peace knowing that your life was spent in the service of others. I find comfort in choosing to honor your memory in the service of others. Even if someone told you that you would be dead seven days later, I know you would still choose to volunteer your last weekend on earth, sharing your faith with those teenagers. You lived your life filled with a deeper love, a fuller meaning that runneth over and touched us all because you knew what mattered most in life: faith and family. And I have no doubt that the source of this was the love you had for God. Here it is, twenty years since the day we met, and you are still teaching me things . . . and will continue to for the rest of my life. Every day of your life was a gift to others. Thank you for reminding me of that. Yes, my Love, I remember now. I see the proof of this is in the love you gave me, our children, and so many others during your lifetime. Now, we will go and do the same. We will go and be a gift for others.

The acceptance and care for the widows as the marginalized are sadly and sorely lacking in faith communities. I was so saddened by the lack of support I received that I decided to mimic the example of a dear friend, Mrs. Andi, by coordinating and facilitating grief support groups (even in the midst of my own grieving). Admittedly, helping others is a step that normally comes much later in the grieving/healing process, which is why it is at the end of the book. However, when the time is right, it is beneficial to our grief healing to help or teach others (even if just in little ways). Naturally, as parents, we are always caring and helping others, but to go out of our way to offer comfort, support, and love to someone else in need is so healing to the giver. For those who already have a job or career in service—nurses, caretakers, teachers, principals, and others—simply do your job in the spirit of love. As a teacher, I always served by giving a smile, offering encouragement, and simply listening to the students, teachers, friends, and parents. When I was tempted to be overcome with exhaustion and hold back my love, I was reminded of Javier's heroic, sacrificial spirit to serve others (despite how tired he felt), and I would choose to love instead. As the old saying goes, "Those who give are the ones who truly receive." I noticed that after I helped others, I always felt better mentally, spiritually, and emotionally.

After getting to a healthier place mentally and emotionally in my grieving process, I found that I wanted to give beyond caring for my own children. It didn't have to be big. Sometimes, the simplest ways of giving (like offering a smile) can create the biggest ripple effect. Along the path of my grieving process, I learned that the saying, "Giving is really a gift to the one who is giving," is absolutely true and wrote this in my journal as a result:

My life is a gift for others. My source of peace is my giving of self.

The most beautiful "gift of self" is to give not just our time, talent, skill, or trade, but it's also in giving simple things like a hug, smile, and kind word. Sometimes, it's in sharing our story, which plants the seeds of faith.

When we are giving in the spirit of love, we are planting a piece of ourselves that comes to fruition within others. Giving to others has been the most profound discovery of healing within my grieving process. Whether it was by volunteering as a parent volunteer for my children's school, singing for my church or at events, creating grief support programs, coordinating retreats, cleaning or cooking for a sick friend, helping our own family members with their children, or even just doing the dishes or picking up a broom for a grieving friend or tired mama, it helped me too. For men (and some women), helping with things like home and car maintenance, lawn care, or teaching skills to children whose fathers are no longer able to teach is invaluable. Like how the boys' Uncle Orlando rose to the opportunity to teach his nephews woodworking, car maintenance, and how to do a proper push-up like a Marine!

After Javier's death, I reached out for support from my student's mother, Cynthia, whose son had passed away suddenly from an illness when he was only sixteen years old. His name was José, and he was the sweetest, meekest boy in our youth group. José often arrived early to chat about his life as I set up and prepped for activities—moments I will cherish forever. After sitting in his room one day and listening to his mom tell me stories of his wrestling action figures, katana sword collection, and even some of the little treasures from the youth group he had saved, Cynthia said it has helped her to talk with me about his life. Here I was thinking I was a burden to her by asking her to listen when all the while, we were giving to each other.

One of my favorite quotes is by St. Mother Teresa of Calcutta, who said, "If you want to change the world, go home and love your family." Such profundity in these words. A few by themselves have the power to change the world, but we all have the power to affect change in the world by loving our families. It's something that sounds so obvious and so simple, yet so many have lost sight of this truth.

My second favorite quote is by a Dutch priest of psychology and social justice, Fr. Henri Nouwen, who said, "Our humanity comes to its fullest bloom in giving." Our love has the power to bear fruit in others and vice versa. When I was not in a position to give and was forced to receive for the sake of my children, tears flooded my eyes because I now knew what it felt like to humbly receive and give *the gift of giving* to the one who is now giving to me. God gives to all living things. In turn, God hopes that we will imitate this selfless love by giving to one another as well. I have personally found this to be the secret to peace—to give out of love. I have felt it deeply on both ends of the spectrum: as a missionary in abundance and giving to the poor and as a humble widow in need of receiving.

I can tell you with a full heart that developing a loving, selfless spirit of giving has saved me from the depths of despair more times than I can count. I now know that giving is the most beautiful part of my spirit because it captures the heart of my beloved Javier. And now, I get to see that same loving, giving spirit in my children as they care for one another, as they care for their little cousins, or as they volunteer in their community. Our hope is that the spark of this giving spirit will spread like wildfire.

Chapter 22

The Ripple Effect

fter I had submitted my manuscript to Morgan James Publishing, I awoke in the middle of the night from a dream of Mrs. Andi facilitating the St. Luke's Grief Support Group. In my dream (which was also a vivid memory), Mrs. Andi smiled at me, took my hand in hers, and comforted me with an indescribable warmth. For you to appreciate the magnitude of love that flowed from Mrs. Andi, I will need to share a bit of who she was to me and how she affected my life.

The most loving thing Mrs. Andi ever said to me was after witnessing our wedding ceremony. As Javier and I blubbered through our wedding vows, faces soaked with messy tears, she said, "I have never seen a couple *so joyous*, so happily in love as you two!" Mrs. Andi wasn't just my neighbor across the street, my mom's best friend, and an active member of my church, she was also my high school counselor. She was always kind to all of her students, with a smile that lit up the hallways. She always encouraged me to succeed, especially as a freshman in the big high school. Her influence upon me often steered me out of trouble with one glance and encouraged me to gain confidence, to excel not only academically but also in my church, in school sports (varsity soccer, the cross-country running team, and community softball team), while acting and singing in performances, and in BPA (Business Professionals of America), where we presented speeches in front of judges and also worked the second half of the day in corporations. I worked in the Accounting department at ExxonMobil Corporation in downtown Houston.

In 2013, I bumped into Mrs. Andi, who had now stepped up to the calling of facilitating my grief support group (the only grief group in my entire area). As I walked into the room, I will never forget her loving welcome: "Juuuulie!" Her face lit up with smiling eyes as she outstretched her arms to receive and embrace me. The meetings she facilitated were healing to everyone because we could feel her wisdom, love, and warmth.

One particular day, as I shared my raw, unfiltered pain, she took my hand in hers, smiled at me, and told me with her loving voice, "You're not alone, Julie. God is going to carry you through this." I normally wasn't receptive to people who told me that God was carrying me, but that day (for some reason), I believed her. Several meetings later, Mrs. Andi shared her own grief and sorrow after recently losing her mother. We had sat there week after week, as she lovingly helped us to carry the burdens of our grief, and all the while, unknown to us, she was carrying the burden of her own mother's death. She had never said a word.

Her example of faith magnified my own faith and hope. I felt she was a hero, and eventually, I mimicked Andi's example to lead grief support groups when I felt strong enough to do so. Our dear, beloved Andi is now in Heaven with my Javier. Andrea Longoria, grandmother of nine and mother of four, was tragically struck and killed by a car while crossing the street on her daily evening walk. The ripple effect of love that flowed from Andi's life upon this earth has affected innumerable lives. I do not understand why Javier and Andi died in the tragic ways they did, but I am grateful for the ripple effect their love had for so many people along this journey of life. Thank you, Mrs. Andi, for answering the call to put love into action. I would not be the mother, daughter, sister, teacher, friend, and overall woman I am today had it not been for your impact upon my life. I love you.

Chapter 23

Acceptance

A question I am often asked is, "How can you keep your faith?"

The answer is, "Every day, I struggle with the choice to keep it." For me, initially, it seemed incomprehensible to trust in an all-powerful, all-loving God, whose divine plan would allow Javier to horrifically die in an explosion the way that he did. To blindly "fully rely on God." How can I trust and "fully rely" on someone who seems to have forgotten about Javier, his wife, his children, his parents, and his siblings? I have had years to grapple with this question. The truth is, the following two words are by far the hardest words I will ever type: "I accept." I accept that this is my life. I accept that the father of my children, my husband Javier, is dead. I cannot understand God's plan, but I can choose to accept it. To totally surrender and fully rely on God is perhaps the hardest obstacle in life for those who have suffered. To paradoxically choose to hold onto faith, hope, and love despite the blinding, crippling tribulations of life's dark storms seems foolish or even ludicrous.

There are two people who helped influence my decision to accept. The first person is Fr. T.J. Martinez, Jesuit president of Cristo Rey Jesuit College Preparatory High School, where I was teaching Theology when Javier died. A memory I have often thought about was the final time Fr. T.J. saw my husband alive. While working late, my husband stopped by the high school with our children to bring me dinner. Fr. T.J. noticed them and stopped in to say hello. In regard to my acceptance, the reason I often think of this memory of Fr. T.J. walking into my classroom to meet my little family is during that joyous interaction we shared, I had no way of knowing that both my husband and Fr. T.J. would soon be in Heaven. The last time I ever saw Fr. T.J. was when he came to visit me at my home a few days after Javier died. He was so kind and compassionate in trying to console me, especially since he had just met Javier and our children. He reminded me of God's love when he said, "His (Javier's) life was a gift. All of our lives are gifts. The question is, what will we do with this gift?" Fr. T.J. helped me to see that after all, it was God who gifted Javier to me, and me to him. And that what we do with our life is a gift to God. Who am I to turn to the same one who provided us with this rare, blissful love with a spirit of ingratitude?

The second person is Javier's mother, Esther. One day many years after Javier's death, while chatting as we cleaned the kitchen together, I shared that I was still struggling with my grief. To my surprise, she said she did not struggle to that same depth or intensity. She explained that she believed that each and every soul passing through life has a mission and that as painful as it is, Javier fulfilled his. Her clairvoyance and love for me helped me loosen the grip of non-acceptance that bound me. How could I know that in the end, it was God's gift of Javier's love that would save me—by gifting me with a family whose love would ultimately lead me back to God.

Now that I have endured many years of this crucible, I see that with each mountain-top and valley experience of life I pass through, life is still beautiful because of the miracle of love Javier and I shared. This is the ultimate prayer God has taught me with the gift and story of Javier. Both in his life and in his death, Javier's life was a prayer. A prayer that reminds me of the mysterious, miraculous wonder of the love of God each time I see his face within the faces of our children, in the way he loved his family, and in the selfless way he served others.

SECTION 5:
Conclusions

Chapter 24

Widows are Among
the Marginalized

**The following chapter is for pastors and leaders
of faith communities who want to better
understand and care for the widow.**

I have painted a vivid picture of my faith to illuminate the fact that not only has my personal faith seen me through my darkest days, but also, I would never want to give any impression of disbelief. As a unique voice, I feel called to both advocate for the widow and help others understand the widow's perspective. That being said, I would like to address how, in addition to the weight of societal and cultural pressures hindering the widow's natural grieving process, there can also be an equally heavy weight of religious pressure upon the widow. Having facilitated and partaken in various ministries over the years, specifically grief support groups throughout my experience as a young widow and my ministry to the widow, I felt saddened with two unexpected, disheartening realizations. First, religious ideologies can inadvertently become a hindrance to our healthy grieving responses by discouraging, judging, or coercing widows from freely feeling all of their natural emotions. Second, widows are deeply misunderstood by all, including their faith communities. This is not a simple statement. It is a tremendously heavy one. For an entire group of people within a religious community to be misunderstood, unknown, isolated, marginalized, considered spiritually weak, and in desperate need of spiritual and physical care is a sad reality. I not only felt hopeless in my faith community, but I also felt *homeless*. For many, our religious community is our "home away from home;" however, after reaching out in need and finding there was no place for me in my "home away from home," I felt more lost than ever. I discovered that what's needed is an understanding of those who mourn and for faith communities to take action to provide care and support for the grieving—namely, with support groups, counselors, pastoral support, practical support, and more.

As for the former, the universal, supreme teaching of Christianity is to focus on the resurrection rather than the suffering and death of Christ. After a deep loss, religious undertones aim to console those who are mourning by convincing the widow to immediately and cheerfully accept their dearly departed's resurrection. For example, many people will coerce widows to focus on their beloved spouse "dancing in the clouds with God," or say, "They're no longer in any more pain," or, "They're in a better place," or "It's all part of God's plan." These religious undertones implicitly or explicitly pressure the widow to immediately accept their spouse's death before they ever had a chance to grieve their loss without any consideration whatsoever as to what place the widow is in their grief process. It's as if the widow is expected to skip right over any "negative" emotions (anger, despair, depression, denial, or unforgiveness) and plunge straight into the acceptance stage of grief.

Due to this leaden expectation from leaders and spiritual mentors, I felt an overwhelming pressure to be a champion of strength in my faith and never appear weak. This constant pressure to heroically uplift others while ignoring my own suffering not only prevented me from healthily grieving, it eventually and unconsciously caused my spirituality and faith life to become stagnant. The amount of energy I spent suppressing my grief to uplift those around me inadvertently caused an aversion toward that which I loved and needed most: my faith. As I said before, the best way to help widows is by allowing them to be in the safety of your presence, to allow them to feel all that they need to feel while walking alongside them throughout the process.

As far as addressing the latter, it's as simple as hearing the plight of the widow by learning what their spiritual and physical needs are. To say I was disheartened after learning there was nothing in my area for widows is a gross understatement. Friends at church didn't even know how to speak to me, so they avoided me altogether. The loneliness that ensued was paralyzing. After wearily going from church to church seeking comfort and acceptance, one particular day, I saw the church parking lot full of cars for a pastoral meeting taking place. As I walked by and looked at the room full of people, I wished so strongly that it was a room full of grieving people so that I could walk in and be received and understood— as well as receive and understand in return. Though I recognized my faith to be the super glue that held me together throughout my life, I couldn't help but share in the emotions of anger and frustration that Jesus felt when he overturned the tables inside the temple. Perhaps I was angry because I had lost so much already. After pondering this conundrum, I told a friend, "I understand Jesus's frustration when he went crashing through the synagogue doors and just 'went temple' on everybody! Throwing over tables right and left in angry frustration toward all the church guys whose focus was more on money than the true mission of God: loving and caring for those in need. I relate to Jesus in that strong emotion of anger, frustration, and disappointment. I mean, it's understandable Jesus flipped out. He saw injustice in the upside-down priorities of the people in that temple, and it made him angry and frustrated. Immediately after Jesus flipped those tables, he healed those in need of healing."

When widows "seek comfort and solace from our home away from home," we may feel as though the Church has turned her back on us. In short, this lack of *Caritas* (charitable love) is isolating because it can feel like a form of betrayal that causes many who are grieving to wrestle with their religiosity. If we can coordinate impressive events, like church festivals, we can likewise have resources available for the hurting members of the community, something with counseling and grief support contact information. At the very least, give a warm embrace, take their phone number, and do what you can to find out what they need. In short, I ask: are the needs of those who mourn just as important as business affairs?

So what can we do to be more inclusive of those who mourn? The first word that pops into my head is *mindfulness*. We, as a faith community, can be ever mindful of the spiritual and physical needs of the poorest, weakest ones. My hope is that leaders will remember the *anawim* of the flock (Hebrew word meaning "little ones, marginalized"). After all, a pastor is a shepherd whose duty to his flock is to seek out and care for the weakest sheep, even if this means he must leave the ninety-nine others in search of "the one." And when he finds the one sheep on the outskirts, lost, scared, injured, and malnourished, he lovingly lays it around his neck and upon his shoulders and carries it all the way back to the safety and comfort of the flock to be cared for and comforted by his brethren. Then, the shepherd joyfully calls all of his friends and says, "Rejoice with me, I have rescued my lost sheep!" (Luke 15:1–7).

Chapter 25

Death Do Us Part—
Dating After Survival Mode

I debated whether to include this chapter. I took it out a dozen times and then put it back a dozen plus one times. I know what you might be thinking; *why is there even a section on dating in a widow's survival book?* But I decided to add this small section to help those widows who are considering it. For those who feel anger or pain from this chapter, I understand. It is not meant for you right now and is only meant to help those who need it. Simply put down the book and come back to it when—*if*—you're ready.

I remember the first time anyone mentioned dating to me after my Javier had died. It not only infuriated me, I felt sick to my stomach! I was physically nauseous with the thought of showing affection to another man. Javier was all I'd ever known! My first real boyfriend I ever French kissed! My first real everything! Years later, I discovered widows are human. Humans in endless pain who badly want to be loved because we (better than anyone) believe in the profound power of true love. We also want our pain and loneliness to subside, and some discover how the distraction of "new love" can feel like a welcomed respite. In good conscience, I feel called to share my personal experience with this.

When I began to group-date with friends after Javier's death, I found that either I was eons ahead of thirty-year-old men in maturity, wisdom, and selflessness or they were intimidated by the experience I had survived (and perhaps even the inner-strength illumined within me). Something I wish someone had told me was how people who feel the endless pain of grief for months and months on end can unknowingly welcome any distraction from their pain, even the giddy feelings of infatuation or "new love." Had I known, maybe then I would not have wasted time and energy by being with those who were not meant for me. However, I do not consider any of the time spent learning these lessons as a loss. God has taught me the most in the lessons of my failures and mistakes.

One lesson I learned in dating after Javier's death was how people who have experienced trauma will often bond with others who have likewise been through trauma. It is understandable since widows deeply long to be understood and accepted. Especially after encountering the myriad of young bachelors (or bachelorettes) who are oftentimes ill-equipped and maybe even afraid to be with a widow. (This is something that makes us widows detest our situation all over again).

Despite knowing that every widow must choose their own unique ways to grieve, I had no idea what this might look like in a relationship. It has taken me years of growth and healing to learn that when people have not processed their trauma and grief, it can manifest in self-destructive behaviors, which affect relationships. I had to learn that no matter how big my heart is, I do not have the power to save or change those who are struggling with these self-destructive or abusive behaviors (such as alcoholism, workaholism, and others). I have also learned it is not my job to teach others how to treat other human beings, how to love people properly, how to be a good parent to their children, and how to healthily grieve. However, the hardest lesson of all was learning that I cannot force nor beg anyone to possess the desire to even want to work on the relationship. Nor can I force anyone to develop the basic tools to do so—namely, self-awareness, communication, trust, empathy, and understanding. Just as widows cannot force someone to have a good heart, we likewise cannot force someone to *not* take advantage of our emotional, mental, and financial vulnerability. Had I known there are men (and women) out there who seek to take advantage of widows in every aforementioned way, I would have been spared an immense amount of pain. Widows are sometimes so hopeful to find love again that they find it profoundly difficult to walk away from those who take advantage of us. However, with self-awareness and faith, we can.

Another obstacle for widows who begin dating is judgment. The sting of judgmental stares and the harsh opinions of family, friends, co-workers, and faith communities were one of the most painful experiences I endured. I was twenty-nine years old and incredibly lonely; however, group dates with friends or being seen with a man prompted everyone in my life to feel compelled to offer their opinions about my behavior, multiplying my pain.

I have said several times that the greatest gift we can give our children is our own healthy mental states. This starts with healing from our past trauma (even generational trauma) to be able to stand firm on our own two feet so we're not easily affected by the judgmental opinions of others. Ultimately, it was better for the widow to find some sort of peace in learning to live life as a single person rather than leaning on a toxic relationship as a crutch to uphold our wounded mental health. Our healing is our responsibility. As I mentioned previously, if we are empty, we are unable to give. The only way to maintain a balanced and healthy mind is to nourish it with a diet of stable, emotional love and care of self.

Javier's selfless love for me reminded me that true love starts with us. It starts with our capacity to know our immeasurable value and self-worth. I wish someone had told me this years ago; then, I may not have wasted my time with men not meant for me. I would have loved myself enough to know who I am and what is best for me. I'd have found a love of reciprocity. A love of teamwork. A love that builds one another up in the most wholesome, complementary way.

A love that is always working and striving toward creating a life of faithfulness rooted in unconditional love for God first and for one another second. Personally speaking, a good partner is a person who puts the will of God and his family above their own needs. I have found that each time I sought true love from a man who did not know how to do this, he did not have the capacity to give the selfless, unconditional love I needed.

Once this true love is found, it is indeed a love worth fighting for!

Stay Connected with Julie

Thank you for reading *A Widow's Hope*

Website: widowshope.net

Facebook: Julz Hope

Instagram: @Julzhopez

TikTok: @widowshope (name: Julzy Hopes)

About the Author

*J*ulie Anne Escalante Ortiz is a mother, teacher, musician, writer, and public speaker. She is the mother of three beautiful children: Daniella, Gabriel, and Tony. She was born and raised in Houston, Texas.

Julie received a scholarship from Our Lady of the Lake University in San Antonio, where she met her late-husband, Javier Ortiz, during her freshman year in college, when she was just eighteen years old. She earned her degree in Theology from the University of St. Thomas in Houston. She has since used her degree to impact the youth community as a missionary, youth pastor, high school Theology teacher, guitar and voice teacher, Spanish teacher, and girls' soccer coach.

As youth pastors for five years at St. Frances Cabrini Church, Julie and Javier led a group of over two-hundred youth per year (equating to thousands of lives). She wrote and directed plays for the youth, taught guitar lessons, sang for her congregation, gave motivational public speeches, and started the Memorial Scholarship Award program in memory of Javier for graduating seniors. Julie also volunteers at countless youth retreats (one of which Javier volunteered for seven days before his death), marriage retreats, and grief ministry retreats.

Julie is currently the high school Latin and Theology teacher for the Archdiocese of Austin. While solo-parenting her three beautiful children, Julie continues to coordinate and facilitate grief support for the widowed community, perform by sharing her singing, and support others in their grief by sharing her story publicly.

Julie is currently working on her second book. For more information, see the section called *Stay Connected with Julie*.

A free ebook edition is available with the purchase of this book.

To claim your free ebook edition:

1. Visit MorganJamesBOGO.com
2. Sign your name CLEARLY in the space
3. Complete the form and submit a photo of the entire copyright page
4. You or your friend can download the ebook to your preferred device

Print & Digital Together Forever.

| Snap a photo | Free ebook | Read anywhere |